MYSTERIES
OF THE OLD WEST

MYSTERIES OF THE OLD WEST

TRUE STORIES FROM THE WILD WEST

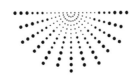

E.B. WHEELER

Rowan Ridge
Press

ISBN: 978-1-960033-01-7

First printing: June 2022

Published by Rowan Ridge Press, Utah

Cover and interior design © Rowan Ridge Press Cover image by

breakermaximus via Deposit Photos

 Created with Vellum

CONTENTS

For everyone who likes a good mystery

NOTE FROM THE AUTHOR

The stories contained in this book are true, based on the most reliable historical and modern sources I could find (you can see a list of some of the main sources for each chapter in the back of the book). I used personal accounts as much as possible, especially for the dialogue of conversations. Sometimes, I had to guess exactly what people said, did, or thought, but I based my guesses on the information we have available. I hope you enjoy trying to solve each mystery!

EMPTY VILLAGES IN THE CLIFFS

On a bitterly cold December day in 1888, two cowboys, Richard Wetherill and Charles Mason, set out to look for lost cattle on the tablelands of southwest Colorado. Their horses pressed on through a steady snowfall. They were on Ute Indian lands, but Richard Wetherill was friends with the local Native Americans. He spoke Ute and Navajo and was allowed to graze his cows on the Ute's "mesas:" the Spanish word for "table," which was what the high, flat land resembled. The cowboys wouldn't find their cattle that day, but the discovery they made would be much more important, and more mysterious.

The wind whipped ice and snow around the two cowboys as they rode.

"I can't feel my feet," Richard called.

Charles nodded. His fingers were stiff and numb with cold. They dismounted and led their horses through the storm to get the blood moving in their limbs and avoid frostbite. Richard and Charles walked to the edge of the mesa, which overlooked the cliffs of the opposite canyon wall. The wintery scent of ice and pinyon pine rode on the wind. As they gazed, the curtain of snow parted and Richard cried out, grabbing Charles's arm. An entire city of stone houses appeared on the side of the steep cliff across from them, sheltered under a huge ledge and guarded by walls and towers.

Cliff Palace as Charles and Richard might have seen it.
Image courtesy of septembergirl via Deposit Photos.

"It looks just like a palace," Charles whispered. If Richard hadn't seen it too, Charles would have thought it was a hallucination brought on by cold and exhaustion.

The canyons harbored the ruins of stone houses, but the cowboys had never seen anything like this. A Ute leader, Acowitz, had told Richard stories about ancient stone villages hidden in the canyons, but he'd also warned them that the cliff houses were sacred places—possibly even cursed—and that the Ute did not visit them.

Richard and Charles were too amazed to worry about curses. They left their horses and searched for a way down the steep canyon walls to the cliff palace on the other side. They managed to scramble over fallen boulders and down old rock slides to reach the bottom of the canyon. The cliff walls were steep, and there was no clear path up to the ruins, especially with the storm blasting them with sharp, cold snow.

It would be easy to give up or try to come back another time. Richard's brother Alfred had once described seeing a cliff palace like this one from the canyon floor, but he'd never been able to find it again. Many of the smaller cliff houses had been destroyed by Spanish miners looking for lost Indian gold or thieves hoping to sell ancient Indian artifacts. Was it possible that this immense village had stayed hidden in the canyons for hundreds of years? It could hold ancient treasures or even answers about the mysterious people who once lived in the canyons.

Richard and Charles wouldn't give up yet. They searched the canyon until they found a way to climb to the mesa on the other side. From there, they backtracked until they stood above the cliff palace. They couldn't see anything below them: there was no hint that an immense village waited just under their feet. Unless the ancient people could fly, though, they had to have a way in and out of their cliff palace. Richard and Charles searched the edges of the mesa.

"Here!" Charles gestured.

Deeply worn stone steps cut along the cliff toward the cliff palace. They were carved from the cliff itself, camouflaged among the rocks. Was it possible that Richard and Charles were the first in hundreds of years to discover them? Clinging to the canyon walls, the two cowboys followed the steps down into the shelter of the cavern that held the cliff palace.

In the protection of the overhang, the storm could not touch them. The city in the cliff was warm, still, and dry. Each step they took raised clouds of powdery dirt. They inhaled it and coughed, imagining the dust of ancient people sticking in their lungs. No other footprints disturbed the ground. Nothing living had passed that way for hundreds of years.

"It feels like someone's watching us," Richard said.

Charles nodded. "Ghosts." There were no signs of life except an old buzzard nest, and even those birds had abandoned the cliff palace.

View of Keet Seel ruins. Photo courtesy of the National Park Service.

Richard and Charles crept along. The silent buildings, several stories tall, sat along streets, connected like apartments. The stones were held together with mortar made of mud, and they could still see the fingerprints of the long-vanished people who built the palace. Some of the fingerprints were large like theirs, but other were small, perhaps belonging to women, and others were so tiny only children could have made them. Everyone worked together to create this amazing refuge in the cliffs. But what had happened to them?

The cowboys carefully poked their heads into some of the rooms. Pots with black and white designs waited on floors and tables, still holding cobs of corn or unfinished weaving. Cooking implements sat by the ashes of fires, ready to make dinner. In one room, it looked like a child had been playing house with pots and stone tools. Everything appeared as if the people had just stepped outside for a moment, planning to return. Or had to flee for their lives without even taking food or a knife for protection.

A pitcher found in Mancos Canyon, Colorado near Cliff Palace. Photo courtesy of the Brooklyn Museum.

"This is strange." Richard pointed to the ceiling. "You can see holes where there were rafters, but the wood is gone."

"If it had rotted, the cloth and corn cobs wouldn't have survived either. Maybe there was a fire?"

"The walls aren't black."

Every room was the same: someone had pulled out all the wooden rafters, but left everything else in place. Did they take it somewhere to make a bonfire, perhaps to keep warm or to send a signal for help or as a warning? Did they intend for their buildings to collapse after they left?

In some of the rooms, the ancient inhabitants had left paintings in red on the wall. One showed pyramids with what looked like an open book or weaving pattern above it, but as far as anyone knows, the ancient Americans didn't have books, and the nearest pyramids are far to the south in Mexico. Other paintings might show lunar events. The ancient people probably studied the stars and the sky to know when the best times were to plant and harvest crops.

Prehistoric red pictographs from Snake Gulch, Arizona.
Photo courtesy of YAYImages via Deposit Photos.

Two unusual rooms were left unfinished. One was round, in contrast to the rectangular rooms in the rest of the cliff palace. The cowboys marveled at how smooth the circular walls were, despite the simple stone tools the ancient people used. The other unfinished room was huge compared to all the others. But what were these projects meant to be? Maybe they served a religious purpose, or were supposed to be a final defense against whatever enemy drove the people from the cliffs.

In the front of Cliff Palace there were large, round structures that extended underground. Richard and Charles recognized that they were similar to the kivas that the modern Pueblo people of Arizona and New Mexico used for religious ceremonies, suggesting a link between the cultures. The ancient Puebloans may have used the kivas the same way, or maybe they were just important gathering places.

View inside Cliff Palace with a round kiva near the center. Photo courtesy of nyfelidae via Deposit Photos.

Yet some of the kivas were filled with trash like broken

pottery and animal bones. Why would a people turn an important gathering place—especially a religious one—into a trash heap? Had they argued over their leadership or religion? Or was it their enemies who had done this?

Behind the buildings, Richard and Charles found a large open space. In one area, there were many stones for grinding grain into flour. Another part was covered in dried bird droppings, but with no signs of birds or nests in the ceiling above.

"I bet they kept turkeys," Charles said, "like the Pueblo Indians do today."

Dwellings of Zuni Pueblo people, some of the possible modern descendants of the ancient cliff dwellers. Photo courtesy of John K. Hillers.

Richard and Charles also found a trash heap and a burial ground. But the burial ground wasn't the only place they found dead bodies. Some were left among the ruins. Had they died defending their homes from invaders, or were these the bodies of the enemies? It seemed clear that someone attacked the cliff palace, but who were they, and why did they leave food and so many valuable goods behind?

Richard and Charles left with more questions than answers. They spent the rest of their lives studying the cliff dwellings and advocating for more protection for the ruins so treasure hunters didn't steal the pots and other artifacts. They learned to conduct archeological digs to discover more about these ancient people, whom the Navajo called "Anasazi," or "ancient enemies." They discovered shells from California and feathers from Mexico in the ruins, showing that the cliff dwellers had traded with other cultures. They found carved channels and stone basins that the ancient people used to collect water during droughts.

Despite the many discoveries made by Richard and Charles, as well as later scientists, the fate of the cliff dwellers remains a mystery.

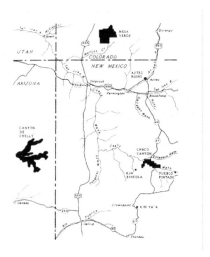

The Four Corners region of the Southwest, including Colorado, New Mexico, Arizona, and Utah, is home to many Ancestral Pueblo ruins. This map from the National Park Service shows some of the biggest sites.

Acowitz warned Richard Wetherill to stay away from the places of the dead. Wetherill was too curious about the past to listen, and for many years, he continued exploring and excavating the cliff dwellings along with his brothers. Then, his luck took a turn for the worse. He had wanted the government to take more of a role in preserving the cliff dwellings, but as they did, they forbade him from doing any more of the research he loved, and he lost the credit for much of his own work.

Struggling to support his family, Richard ended up opening a trading post in New Mexico. There, one of his Navajo customers ambushed and shot him for reasons that were never clear. Had the ghosts of the past finally caught up with him for disturbing the secrets of the dead?

2

ESTEBAN THE MOOR AND THE SEVEN CITIES OF GOLD

A Spanish friar, Marcos de Niza, pushed north from the settlement of New Spain in Mexico, venturing into the deserts of the American Southwest. The landscape was barren, with little water or food, but Marcos pressed on under the burning sun. He was chasing a legend: the Seven Cities of Cibola, also known as the Cities of Gold. Rumors had reached the Spanish in Mexico about native cities with silver-lined streets and chieftains who fell asleep each night to the sound of hundreds of tiny golden bells. The Spanish wanted these riches for themselves.

More than the heat or lack of food and water, one thing made Marcos truly uncomfortable. He was the official head of this 1539 expedition, but he knew its true leader was a Black slave called Estevanico, or Esteban the Moor, and he wasn't sure if Esteban could be trusted.

Esteban had gained fame in Mexico as one of the first non-natives to trek across much of America, along with his master and two other Spaniards. Now, as he led the way back into the deserts of the Southwest, members of the local tribes flocked around him, offering gifts and joining him on his journey. They treated him like a modern movie star. He spoke their language and understood their culture. If anyone could guide the Spanish to the Cities of Gold, it was Esteban. But would Esteban stay loyal to the Spanish?

He traveled ahead of Fray Marcos and the main party. Fray Marcos didn't like this arrangement, but he couldn't keep up with Esteban, who was strong and fit after spending eight years walking hundreds of miles.

Esteban had arranged a way to tell Marcos about the villages he encountered: if the place he found had only a little wealth, he would send a small cross back with one of the Sonoran Indians who had come with them from Mexico. If the village was very wealthy, he would send a larger one. As Marcos trudged onward into what is now New Mexico, one of the Sonorans brought back a cross as tall as a man.

Marcos looked at it in amazement. Did this mean Esteban had discovered the cities of gold? Marcos hurried forward, despite sore feet and a mouth aching for water. In the distance, he saw a settlement. The two- and three-story buildings looked golden in the sunlight—better than anything he had dreamed of.

As he rushed toward unimagined wealth, he met the rest of Esteban's scouting party. They ran toward him, their eyes wide with terror.

"What are you doing?" Marcos asked.

The Sonorans gestured to the city in the distance. "The

Zuni of Hawikuh! They accused Esteban of being a spy and captured him. They will kill him, and then they'll kill us!"

A Zuni city in the 1800s. Image courtesy of the British Library.

Marcos hesitated, torn between longing for the golden city, and fear of the Zuni. Fear won. Marcos fled to Mexico, but he told everyone he had glimpsed the City of Gold in the distance. No one in the party ever bothered to find out what had actually happened to Esteban.

The next year, in 1540, the Spanish conquistador Coronado traveled north in search of Cibola. Though he ventured far into modern America and heard many amazing stories, he never found golden cities. Where did these legends come from, and did Esteban know the truth?

———

Imagine leaving behind your home, your friends and family, your language and your beliefs, and even your name. That's what happened to Esteban when he was young. He was born in Morocco, in northern Africa around the year 1500, just eight years after Christopher Columbus reached the Americas. He was a Moor: a black African Muslim. At the time that he was born, his city was under the control of the Portuguese, and at some point, he was taken to Spain as a slave. His real name was not Esteban—that was the name given to him by his masters—but they did not record his birth name. Maybe he never told them.

There are no existing portraits of Esteban, but several artists have tried to imagine how he might have looked. Image courtesy of David Weber Collections.

He became the slave of a man named Andres Dorantes. This would have been bad enough, but Dorantes's family were relatively poor. Dorantes, caught up in the gold fever of his age, decided to set sail for the mysterious land of Florida under the command of Captain Narvaez. The men hoped to claim the land for Spain, start a colony, and find the legendary riches of the unknown lands of North America.

They could not have imagined the dangers that awaited them—only four of the 600 men would finish their journey.

Did Esteban look forward to this adventure? He may have seen it as an opportunity for a new life, but he would be sailing far from his home, and he would still be a slave. Yet if there was hope anywhere for Esteban to be free, it would have been in the "New World" of the Americas.

The expedition set out from Spain in 1527 with five ships. The party included soldiers, sailors, servants, slaves, and the wives of the married men. It took a couple of months to sail across the Atlantic Ocean to the Caribbean island of Santa Domingo. While there, they heard rumors of another expedition where only 150 of the original 600 men survived. More than 140 of the soldiers deserted on the spot. Esteban stayed. Maybe he wanted to take his chances with Dorantes in Florida, or maybe Dorantes kept watch over him so he couldn't run.

They sailed on for the island of Cuba. It was supposed to be a safe place where they could get supplies for their journey. While they were there, though, a storm came up. Esteban had never seen such fierce winds, tearing up trees and sending monstrous waves crashing into the island as if the ocean would swallow them whole. It was a hurricane, and when it was over, they found pieces of some of their boats stranded in the tops of the surviving trees. Sixty sailors had drowned trying to save the ships.

They had not even reached Florida, and had already lost two ships, 200 men, and many of their horses and supplies. Captain Narvaez decided to spend the winter in Cuba, but the lure of fame and fortune still called, and in the spring, they sailed for Florida.

In April, almost a year after leaving Spain, Esteban finally saw the west coast of Florida: a flat, thickly forested land of many swamps. There, the Spanish leaders went ashore and announced—in Spanish, which none of the Native Americans understood—that Florida was now a part of Spain, and the Native peoples should obey them or prepare for war.

The expedition raided one of the villages and found large nuggets of gold. Esteban and the others felt new energy at the sight of the precious metal. Wasn't this what they had hoped for?

Captain Narvaez held the gold out to the villagers and asked, "Where did you get this? Where can I find more?"

The villagers understood what he wanted. They pointed north and said, "Apalachee."

It would have been safer to stay with the ships, but Captain Narvaez, in his hunger for wealth, left them behind to march straight north. None of them ever saw the ships again.

Esteban was forced to march with the others; there was no turning back. They did find larger, richer settlements to the north, but there was no gold for the easy taking. This northern tribe, the Apalachee, were skilled warriors. To Esteban and the others, they seemed as tall and strong as giants, and they could shoot a bow with such force that the arrow would go all the way through a tree. The arrows could certainly pierce Spanish armor.

Running low on food and fresh water, the expedition

retreated with the Apalachee on their trail. Esteban and the others trudged through swamps as high as their chests, being bitten by mosquitoes and dragged down by their heavy armor. The Apalachee attacked them as they went, and the Spanish couldn't shoot their guns when they were nearly drowning in swamp water.

A Florida swamp like those that Esteban had to cross. Photo courtesy of wildnerdpix via Deposit Photos.

Finally, the expedition made their way to a river. The mosquitoes had given them malaria, which caused them to shiver and ache with fever. They had run out of food, every one of them was injured, and their ships were gone. Esteban sat on the shore and wondered if he was going to die.

"There's only one way to survive," the men said. "We must build ships and sail away."

One man came forward. "I know how to made wooden pipes and deerskin bellows. Perhaps we could melt down our stirrups, spurs, crossbows—anything made of iron—to make tools."

"We can eat the horses," someone else suggested.

Another man said, "I can make pitch from pine sap to hold the pieces of the boats together."

With the local tribes constantly attacking and many of their people dying from malaria, Esteban and the others set to work building five barges. Esteban had never eaten horse meat, but he was so hungry, he wolfed it down without tasting it. By the time they sailed away from Florida, there were just under fifty people crammed into each small boat— less than 250 of the original 600 men. None of them knew how to sail, and it was hurricane season again.

Captain Narvaez took the strongest men in his boat. Esteban's chance of survival would be best with the captain, or in the boat of the clever officer Cabeza de Vaca, but he had to stay with his master Dorantes in a different boat.

The men had just a little raw corn they had stolen from the Native Americans to eat. If they tried to get close to shore, the native tribes living along the coast often attacked them. They only had occasional rain water to drink. Some men became so thirsty that they drank the salt water and died as the salt dried up their organs. Thirst scratched at Esteban's throat, and the water looked deliciously cool and refreshing, but he saw what happened to the others who tried it.

The five boats tried to stay together, but the currents pulled them apart. Cabeza de Vaca thought the men in the boats should try to help each other, but Captain Narvaez, with the strongest sailors, disagreed.

"It's not my job any longer to command you," Narvaez called across the rushing waters. "We must save ourselves, and that's what I'm going to do!"

Narvaez's boat drifted away, never to be seen again.

A statue imagining how Cabeza de Vaca looked. Image courtesy of Ealmagro.

Esteban's boat and Cabeza de Vaca's boat were now the only ones left. The wind blew, a damp, bitter cold that cut through the men's tattered clothes. Cold, ill, and starved, the men began to collapse. Esteban curled up on the floor of the boat, waiting for death.

He was jolted back to consciousness when huge waves slammed the boat. This was the beginning of another hurricane, yet it gave Esteban some hope, for he could hear the waves crashing against land. He and the others who had not frozen or starved to death struggled out of the boat and climbed up the rocky shore to lap rain water off the ground and move about to keep from freezing. They discovered they were on an island, now called Galveston, in Texas. Fortunately for them, it was inhabited by friendly Native Americans who fed and sheltered the starving men.

The Europeans and Africans brought diseases with them, though. The Native Americans had never encountered these illnesses, so their bodies had little resistance to the germs. Soon, half of the Native Americans died. The survivors considered killing the newcomers. By this time, only sixteen of the original 600 men were still alive, including Esteban and his master Dorantes. The few remaining Europeans and Africans survived by agreeing to become slaves to the Native Americans.

Now Esteban was twice a slave. America's promises of riches and freedom dissolved like sea foam. The Native Americans forced Dorantes to work right alongside Esteban, though. Both men dug for food and carried heavy loads of wood. Some of the other survivors of their expedition grew desperate and tried to fight back or run, and the Native Americans killed them. Esteban knew how to work, and he kept his head down and focused on the one hope he could still grasp: survival.

Slowly, Esteban and the others improved their living conditions. Using a combination of Native American and European medicine and superstition, first Cabeza de Vaca, and then Dorantes, Esteban, and a fourth surviving Spaniard named Castillo, began working with the ill Native Americans and had a great deal of success in healing them. They gradually rose from slaves to traders and healers. As they did, they tried to make their way south and west where they would find the Spanish settlements in Mexico.

Esteban suffered and worked alongside the other men, but as their fame grew among the Native Americans, the three Spaniards began to separate themselves from both Esteban and the native people. In order to look like "children of the sun," as the Native Americans believed them to be, they would send Esteban to do errands and work as a go-between. Esteban may have been annoyed or frustrated by this reminder that, after everything he had survived alongside the other men, he was still a slave. It also gave him an advantage, though: no one in the party learned the native languages and customs better than he did.

A map showing Esteban's route through the future United States and Mexico. Image based on the map by Lencer, CC by-SA 3.0.

As they traveled west through the deserts of modern New Mexico, many of the native people gave them gifts, including jewelry and other items made from turquoise and copper, which they said came from the richer lands to the north. Narvaez would have chased the treasures. Maybe, a year or two earlier, Esteban and the others would have too, but now they only wanted to get back to a place where they had regular food and clothing and would be safe.

Finally, their travels brought them to Mexico in 1536, nine years after leaving Spain. Esteban's Spanish companions rejoiced to meet with their countrymen, though they were upset to see how the Europeans were enslaving the native peoples. After living with the Native Americans so long, they were still strangers among the tribes in many ways, but they had also learned to see things differently than their own people did.

What might Esteban have thought about reaching Mexico? In the desert, he was always hungry and often thirsty and tired, but he had a kind of freedom he might not have enjoyed since his childhood in Morocco.

The three Spaniards made plans to travel back to Spain or settle down in Mexico, but Esteban did not have a choice. Back in civilization, his status as slave overwhelmed all his other accomplishments. Dorantes sold him to the Viceroy of New Spain, Antonio de Mendoza. It was as Mendoza's slave that Esteban once again marched north into the lands where he had been not a slave, but a celebrity.

Did Esteban try to warn his masters that he had never seen golden cities in the north, or did he encourage the rumors, hoping for the chance to escape once again from the confines of civilization? When he reached Hawikuh, did he make a fatal error, angering the Zuni and finally bringing about his death in the desert he had once escaped? Or did he make an arrangement with them, slipping away from the eyes of the Spanish and from history?

No records tell us for sure, but one interesting clue remains. The Zuni people have figures known as kachinas that represent the spirits of ancestors and other things in the natural world. One of them is a black kachina with a frightening face named Chakwaina, and many think this kachina represents Esteban. But were the Zuni representing an enemy, or a friend? The secret is lost in the deserts of New Mexico.

A kachina figure. Photo courtesy of ejkrouse via Deposit Photos.

And what about the Cities of Gold? Marcos de Niza claimed to have seen them before fleeing from the Zuni, but when he traveled with Coronado the year after Esteban's disappearance, there was no trace of the golden cities he remembered. Had he seen the tan-colored adobe pueblos from a distance and thought they were made of gold? Or only imagined what he hoped to find? Legends and rumors of gold and other wealth persisted, but neither Coronado nor modern explorers have ever found a golden city. Still, the stories of riches have left many to wonder if there are treasures hidden in the mountains of the Southwest.

3
THE LOST HAWAIIAN TRAPPERS

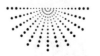

In the wildlands of southwestern Idaho, there are a mountain range and river named Owyhee. The word looks strange, but it's actually just an old spelling of Hawaii. The name commemorates the adventures of the many Hawaiians who left their home to seek their fortune in the Pacific Northwest, and especially of three of the Hawaiians who ventured into the region and were never seen again.

In 1811, the trading ship *Tonquin* approached the waters where the mighty Columbia River of the Oregon Territory meets the Pacific Ocean. The men on board hoped to get rich on the new treasure of the American West: furs. The pelts of North American animals, especially beavers, were very warm and soft and could be sold in China, Europe, America, and other parts of the world for large amounts of money. Twelve of the adventurers on the *Tonquin* were native Hawaiians who had left their tropical home to seek their fortunes and to learn more about the world outside their islands. But before any of them could get rich, they had to get past the Columbia River Bar.

An image of the Tonquin *in calmer waters but under attack by Native peoples. From Edmund Fanning's* Voyages to the South Seas, Indian and Pacific Oceans, China Seas, North-West Coast.

The Columbia River Bar is the area where the cold, fast waters of the Columbia River collide with the Pacific Ocean. Dirt deposited by the river builds up there, causing sandbars that can catch and sink unsuspecting ships. Huge waves roar over these sandbars where the two waters meet. This creates some of the roughest waters in the world and earned the area the name Graveyard of the Pacific for the number of ships it sank.

A storm had battered the *Tonquin* for the last several days, soaking all of the men and sending icy blasts slithering through their coats. The boat rolled heavily from side to side, threatening to toss the men off of the slippery deck and into the grasp of the ocean. The Hawaiians, used to tropical weather, shivered in misery. They could see the shore, but between them and it, mountainous waves crashed over the sandbars, sending geysers of white spray into the stormy sky.

There seemed to be no way through. The captain, Jonathan Thorn, sent a smaller boat out to try to find safe passage, but the waves crushed it and sent the sailors to watery graves.

When the storm eased a little, Captain Thorn said, "We have to send out another boat to guide us through the bar."

The sailors looked at each other and at the rolling waves battering the ship.

Alexander McKay, one of the representatives of the fur company, protested. "It's a death sentence to send a small boat into these waves."

Captain Thorn refused to listen. He looked over the remained crew. His sailors spent their lives on the water, but most of them had never learned how to swim—they were from places where the water was cold and dangerous and no one thought swimming was an enjoyable or healthy activity. The Hawaiians, however, were experienced swimmers, divers, and sailors. Captain Thorn chose two of the Hawaiians to be part of the five-man crew on the second boat.

The sailors lowered the Hawaiians and their shipmates into the rolling waves. The tide grabbed their little boat and pulled them away from the ship, but they rowed through the cold waters rolling around them, guiding the larger ship around the sandbars and toward the shore. When the worst danger seemed to be behind them, the ship caught the wind and sailed past the little boat. The Hawaiians and their crew mates tried to catch up, but the waves tore them away, sending them farther south. A monstrous breaker struck them from the side and tossed the men into the roaring waters.

Swimming through the frigid ocean, the Hawaiians righted the boat, rocked it to dump out much of the water, and pulled themselves on board. They were also able to save one of the white sailors who had managed to stay afloat, and together they bailed out the boat. Unfortunately, the icy waters of the northern Pacific were nothing like the warm ocean around Hawaii, and the damp cold gave them hypothermia. One of the Hawaiians died, but the other survived to rejoin the remaining ten Hawaiians on the shore of the Oregon Territory, the first of many of their fellow Islanders who would join the race to control the fur trade of the Pacific Northwest. Some would return to Hawaii wealthy, but others would disappear into the vast North American wilderness.

This image showing Native Hawaiians battling with European explorers reminds us that the interactions between Europeans and Native peoples was often violent. Image from John Cleveley the Younger.

Once they reached the Oregon Territory, the Hawaiians helped build Fort Astoria on the coast. They worked alongside men from Canada, Scotland, Russia, the United States, Africa, Bengal, China, Japan, and many other parts of the world. Far too often, their names were not recorded, but their contributions were still essential to the exploration of the West. They served as laborers, soldiers, and trappers. Because the Hawaiians had proved their skills as sailors and swimmers, some fur companies required that each of their parties contain at least one Hawaiian to manage canoes on the river. The number of Hawaiians in the Northwest continued to grow, along with the dangers of the fur trader's life.

Those dangers could be considerable. The harsh weather and rugged landscape were just one part of the challenge. Competition between the North West Company, or Nor'Westers, to which the Hawaiians belonged, and their rivals the Hudson Bay Company often turned violent with a series of bloody clashes in the 1810s. The traders were also entangled in the fighting between the native Nez Percé and Shoshone people.

The beaver's warm, water-repellant coat made it so valuable that people risked their lives and fought each other to collect their furs. Photo courtesy of FrankFF via Deposit Photos.

In 1818, a Scotsman with the North West Company named Donald McKenzie set out on a daring mission: to establish a fort far inland, in what is now Washington, near the Idaho border. It would give the Nor'westers an advantage over the Hudson Bay Company, and McKenzie also hoped he could orchestrate a peace between the Nez Percé and Shoshone, which would make it easier for the Nor'Westers to trap and trade furs in the region.

McKenzie was a bulky man—well over 300 pounds—and did not seem well-suited to such a sensitive mission, but he had already explored in the area, and he went to Fort George—as Astoria had been renamed—to find men who would go with him on this journey. He met with the commanders of the fort, who laughed at his idea.

"Your plans are wild," Mr. Keith, one of the commanders, told him. "You'll never succeed, nor do I think any gentleman here will be so foolish as to attempt an establishment on the Nez Percé's lands."

"I've been there already," McKenzie said. "Give me the men and goods I require, and I'll show you."

Keith shook his head. "This is folly and madness. Only disaster will come of it."

McKenzie stormed out and consulted with his friend and fellow trader Alexander Ross.

"You do not know Mr. Keith," Ross warned. "He does everything by the rule book and will risk nothing. You, on the contrary, must risk everything."

Finally, Keith sent McKenzie a note, granting him only a little aid for the trip. McKenzie asked around Fort George for men willing to go with him. Very few of the white men would join such a dangerous mission, but several Hawaiians, as well as Iroquois and Abanakee from the northeast United States, were willing to go with him. They had already ventured this far, and they would take a chance on the inland adventure.

They set out for what is now Washington and began work on Fort Nez Percé. It seemed like a good site because it marked the place where the American explorers Lewis and Clark had signed a peace treaty with some of the native tribes. But that was many years earlier, and the native peoples opposed the new fort. While the Hawaiians worked to cut down trees and build the fort, the local tribes gathered their warriors, threatening to kill all the men there.

McKenzie negotiated with the local chiefs, paying for the right to build the fort on their land. The Hawaiians and other trappers finished their work, established what would be an important trading post and stopping point for westward travelers.

A replica of one of the forts the Hawaiians helped build.
Photo courtesy of Zach Frank via Adobe Stock.

With Fort Nez Percé established, McKenzie wanted to establish peace between the warring Nez Percé and

Shoshone tribes so his men could venture further east and trap and trade in what is now Idaho.

McKenzie, along with some of his Native American, white, and Hawaiian companions, set out to call a council of the Shoshone leaders. The Shoshone were divided into groups who hunted buffalo, groups who fished, and a band called the Ban-at-tees, who lived in the mountains and were considered outlaws by the other groups. It was unusual for all of the bands to meet together and come to an agreement, but McKenzie convinced them to listen to what he had to say.

McKenzie and his companions met with Pee-eye-em, the head chief of the Shoshone. McKenzie was a large man, and the Hawaiians were used to being taller than many of the Native Americans, but Pee-eye-em was over six feet tall and made all of them look tiny in comparison.

"How many Shoshone are there?" McKenzie asked.

He, the Hawaiians, and their other companions were putting themselves in a dangerous situation. If the Shoshone decided to turn against them, they would have to fight their way out, and they would likely lose against a large force of Shoshone.

At first, Pee-eye-em wouldn't answer, but when McKenzie asked again, the chief said, "What makes you ask that?"

"I should like to know in order to tell our father, the great white chief."

"Oh! Tell him, then, that we are as numerous as the stars."

Pee-eye-em might have been exaggerating to discourage

outsiders from attacking his nation, but the gathering of Shoshone consisted of about 10,000 people, who pitched their tents along seven miles of the river. The Nor'Westers were vastly outnumbered and had to hope the peace talks went well.

Fur traders negotiated with many Native leaders to trap beavers on their lands. Image courtesy of Wikimedia.

McKenzie addressed the Shoshone leaders, suggesting a treaty between them and the Nez Perce in order to bring peace and trade to all of the people in the region.

Chief Pee-eye-em pointed to the Ban-at-tee. "These are the people who disturb the peace and wage war with the Nez Percé and plunder the whites. But still, as this treaty is the wish of the whites, and in our interest to get our wants supplied, we cordially agree to it."

Ama-qui-em, Pee-eye-em's brother, turned on the Ban-at-tee present and said, "Yes, you are robbers and murderers too! You have robbed the whites; you have killed the whites." He paused regretfully. "But it is now past. Let us utter it no more. Go then home to your wives and to your children. Rob no more, and we shall all be friends."

They signed the treaty, and the Nor'Westers celebrated along with the Shoshone. But they were still concerned about the Ban-at-tee. The Ban-at-tee were angry at the way the other Shoshone bands spoke to them, and the Nor'Westers could not be sure the Ban-at-tee would keep their part of the peace agreement. The Nor-Westers also had to fear the Hudson Bay Company, who had attacked other Nor'Westers and resented the fort the North West Company had built so far inland.

After the celebrations broke up, the Nor'Westers decided to part ways to trap furs. Three of the Hawaiians turned south, looking for a good river where they could catch beaver.

This map of Oregon, Washington, and Idaho shows the locations of the forts where the Hawaiians worked and the Owyhee region, which was their last known location.

McKenzie's party continued on, but they realized that someone was following them. They traveled faster. Could trappers from the Hudson Bay Company be on their trail? Or had the Ban-at-tee or others of the Shoshone decided to break the treaty and rob them? McKenzie's party tried to shake their pursuit, but the only thing that saved them was the arrival of a massive blizzard.

Now, instead of running from a potential enemy, the trappers were fighting for their lives against nature. The winter storm piled snow so deeply, it reached up to the horses' bellies. In this all-white world created by the storm, a trapper named Hodgens went missing. The main party had to keep moving forward to get to an encampment where they could warm up and wait out the winter storms. They could not search for smaller groups like the Hawaiians or for missing men like Hodgens.

Hodgens had lost the party in the drifts of snow pushing around him like giant waves in an ocean of white. In the confusion, he lost his horse and had to trudge through the freezing cold on foot. The temperature dropped to 20 and even 30 degrees below zero. He tried to start a fire by sparking the gunpowder on his flintlock gun, but the mechanism broke.

Hodgens should not have been able to survive in such grim circumstances, but trappers and mountain men knew they had no one to fall back on for help when things got bad; they had to depend on themselves. Hodgens dragged himself through the snow, weak from lack of food and in danger of freezing to death if he stopped moving. Two weeks after getting lost, he stumbled into a Shoshone encampment. He recognized the tent of the chief Ama-ketsa from the peace negotiations and pushed his way inside.

Ama-ketsa cared for him eleven days until he was well enough to travel, then the Shoshone helped him back to the trapper's camp. The trappers had heard rumors from some of the Shoshone of trouble between trappers and Native Americans during the winter, so they were relieved to see Hogdens again.

Once the winter storms were over, they met up again with some of the smaller parties who had separated before the storm. Still, the Hawaiians did not return to the main encampment, so they set out to find them. McKenzie and his men found their camp, but it had been deserted. A trapper thought he saw one of the Hawaiian's horses with a party of Ban-at-tees. Then, a search turned up a skeleton that might have belonged to one of the men. Faced with' the impossibility of finding anything else in the vast wilderness, McKenzie and his men assumed the Hawaiians had perished during the winter.

The Owyhee River in the wilderness where the Hawaiian trappers went missing. Photo courtesy of YAYImages via Deposit Photos.

Had one of the Shoshone bands such as the Ban-at-tee

broken their treaty and robbed and the Hawaiians, killing them in the struggle or leaving them to freeze? Had the Hawaiians encountered traders from the Hudson Bay Company and fought with them? Or had the desperate winter led them to seek shelter with one of the local tribes as Hodgens had done? Perhaps, like some of the other Hawaiians who came to the Pacific Northwest, they married native women and became part of their tribe.

Though their fate remains a mystery, they left their mark on history through their skill and daring as part of the North West Company and left their mark on the map with the mountain range and river called Owyhee in remembrance of where they went missing.

4

THE MYSTERIOUS WEALTH OF THOMAS RHOADES

Thomas Rhoades was once one of the richest men in the West. He had been present at the discovery of gold at Sutter's Mill in California and made a fortune there, but that might not have been his only source of wealth. His neighbors reported that he would venture off into the mountains of Utah and return with bags of gold. People tried to follow him, but no one was ever able to discover where he found the gold, and some of it might still be hidden in the mountains of Utah.

Before he was wealthy, Thomas Rhoades had pioneered his way west. By the 1840s, American settlers were rolling their wagons across the plains and over trails established by fur trappers. Many followed the Oregon Trail to the Pacific Northwest to settle in Washington and Oregon. Some ventured farther south to California, which was still a part of Mexico at the time.

Members of the Church of Jesus Christ of Latter-day

Saints, sometimes known as Latter-day Saints or Mormons, also forged a western trail in the 1840s. Their beliefs in modern prophets and new scriptures put them at odds with their neighbors in the East. They moved to Missouri until clashes over religion and slavery, which their leader Joseph Smith opposed, led to violence. Mobs killed some of their members and the governor issued an "extermination order" against them. They built a new city in Illinois, called Nauvoo, and for a time it was larger than Chicago. Then Joseph Smith was murdered and an angry horde ransacked their city. The Latter-day Saints fled farther West, hoping to find peace in the Rocky Mountains.

After Joseph Smith's death, Brigham Young became the
"American Moses" who led the Mormon exodus to Utah.

Thomas Rhoades was part of this church, but he didn't stay with the main body of Latter-day Saints. In fact, he had owned slaves and stayed behind in Missouri despite the extermination order. How he did so without being harassed is just one of the mysteries about him. But when the rest of the Latter-day Saints fled for the West, Thomas Rhoades decided he would join them. Instead of going north to Nebraska, where the main body of Latter-day Saints would spend the winter, the Rhoades and several other families headed for California, planning to meet up with the rest of their church later. In fact, the Rhoades family arrived in California in 1846, only a little ahead of the infamous Donner Party, who were stranded in the mountains by an early storm and resorted to eating their dead to survive. Some of the Rhoades family were part of the rescue efforts that finally brought the Donner Party survivors to California.

Having been lucky in avoiding the winter storms, Thomas Rhoades set up house, and he was about to be lucky again, because he settled close to a place that would soon be famous around the world: Sutter's Mill, the birth place of the California Gold Rush.

Early gold prospectors at Sutter's Mill in California. Photo courtesy of Wikimedia.

Rhoades wasn't the only Latter-day Saint in California. A group had sailed on the *Brooklyn* all the way around the tip of South America to come up the coast in an experiment on the best way to travel west. And the group known as the Mormon Battalion also arrived in California in 1847. They had been angry that the government didn't protect their homes and families from the mobs, but they needed money to help them move west, so they joined the US Army to fight in the Mexican-American War. Their long march ended in California, and they made their way north to Sutter's Mill.

The northern route shows the Mormon Trail, following the Oregon Trail and then cutting south to Utah. The southern route is the one taken by the Mormon Battalion along the Santa Fe trail and then across to California.

Some stories claim it was a servant of Rhoades's, Jemima Powell, who found the first gold at Sutter's Mill. In 1848, When James Marshall and a group of men from the Mormon Battalion found the gold that would start the Gold Rush, the Latter-day Saints, already on the scene, had the chance to prospect before the main rush of "Forty-Niners" arrived the next year. Thomas Rhoades quickly became a very rich man.

When the new Latter-day Saint leader, Brigham Young, arrived in the Salt Lake Valley of Utah in 1848 and proclaimed, "This is the right place," many of the California Saints journeyed back to Utah, bringing their gold with them. Thomas Rhoades was one of those men. No one knows exactly how much gold he found, but he had enough money to donate $10,000 worth of gold to Brigham Young and the church when he reached Utah. That's the equivalent of about a quarter of a million dollars today.

Rhoades built a fine house in Salt Lake City and took several important leadership positions in the church and in the new Utah Territory. But family stories and local lore say he had an important job that was never recorded. Chief Wakara of the Ute people had joined the Latter-day Saints, and—stories say—he was prepared to show them the way to an ancient gold mine to help the church. He didn't want everyone tromping through Ute land, so he would reveal the location to just one white man. Thomas Rhoades was the man selected for the job.

Rhoades started a new settlement in Kamas Valley near the Uintah Mountains where this lost mine was supposed to be located. Local legend says he was often seen going into the mountains and returning with bags of gold, though he didn't live like a particularly rich man with a huge house or fancy clothes. He never told anyone about the gold or where he was going until he became too sick to make the journey and passed the knowledge on to his son Caleb. Caleb continued visiting the mines until a later chief, Chief Tabby, declared that no more outsiders were allowed on Ute lands.

A Ute encampment in the Uintahs by Henry Chapman Ford.

In addition to the Ute mine, some also believed that Thomas Rhoades found gold on his own while hunting in the mountains. After all, he had been at Sutter's Mill and knew what to look for. Utah has never had a huge gold rush, but prospectors sometimes found small amounts of gold in the state. Brigham Young might have asked Thomas Rhoades to keep the location of his mines a secret to avoid a gold rush overwhelming Utah. After all, the Latter-day Saints had enough problems with neighbors in the past. They preferred to stay isolated.

Caleb knew about the location of these other mines as well. At one point, he requested that the government give him a land lease in the area of his mine.

"If you give it to me," he said, "I'll pay off the national debt."

Utah representative George Q. Cannon told Congress, "He's only an ignorant prospector."

Congress told Caleb no, and Caleb took whatever he knew about the mines to his grave.

Thomas Rhoades died in 1869. The church leaders wrote an obituary for him, but the newspapers never printed it.

And the obituary simply said that Rhoades was a pioneer and a great grizzly bear hunter. No mention of Sutter's Mill or Ute gold. Perhaps church leaders didn't want people to think of mining and gold rushes.

The Rhoades gold has been said to have been used to mint gold coins for use in Utah and also to have been used to plate the angel statue on top of the temple in Salt Lake City. No one knows for sure the source of the gold. Was there really a lost Spanish mine in the mountains of Utah? Carvings are found in the rocks there that appear to be Spanish, as are old mining equipment that is hard to date. Though the friars Dominguez and Escalante are famous for making a trek through Utah in 1776—the same year the thirteen colonies were fighting for their freedom from Great Britain—they were not the first Spaniards to venture north from Old Mexico. Modern Utes who are willing to talk about the mines don't know for sure if they exist, though many have also heard the stories.

The vast Uintah wilderness may hold lost treasures, but it's a huge area for anyone to search. Photo courtesy of booizzy via Flickr, CC 2.0.

Some think the gold is even older than the Spanish, dating back to the Aztecs. Rumors say that the Aztec ruler Montezuma hid his treasure in Utah to keep the Spanish conquistadors from getting it. Could this be the origin of the stories of the Lost Cities of Gold?

Enough people believe in the gold, including Thomas Rhoades' descendants and descendants of his neighbors, that people are still looking for even now. Gale Rhoades spent his life looking for the treasure. He died of a heart attack while searching for it. After his death, someone broke into his house and stole his maps and papers.

Several other treasure hunters have thought they were close, finding flooded or collapsed caves that might have once been part of the mines, but no one has successfully proven that what they found was the Rhoades mine or even a lost Spanish mine. Several people have died in the attempts to find the mine, and many more have lost their health and their money hunting for it. Some say it is protected by ancient spirits, others think they know where it is if they only had investors willing to pay for the equipment to clear rocks away in the right place. Others think the mines never existed and that Thomas Rhoades had hidden huge amounts of his gold from California in the mountains to protect it from thieves—a cache of wealth that might still be hidden there.

Maybe someday, someone will find the gold and unravel the mystery of Thomas Rhoades's treasure.

5
THE TATTOOED GIRL

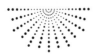

Fifteen-year-old Lorenzo Oatman woke in the Arizona desert with a headache pulsing behind his eyes. Blood matted his hair. He groaned and pushed himself up, trying to remember. The memories of war cries and screams crowded out everything else.

He climbed out of the gully where he had awoken. Nearby, he spotted another figure on the ground. His mother. Her eyes stared at the cloudless sky, unseeing, and blood stained the sand beneath her. Someone had lined more of his family up beside her in a neat row: his father and his brothers and sisters. All dead. Only two of his sisters, eleven-year-old Mary Ann and fourteen-year-old Olive, were missing from the gruesome lineup.

Lorenzo staggered to his feet, needing to get away. What had happened? His family had been trying to get to California. The group they were traveling with had stopped in Arizona, but his father decided to press on alone. They had encountered a group of Yavapai, who had tried to negotiate with Royce for supplies. When Royce wouldn't sell to them, the Yavapai attacked.

His head spinning with pain and thirst, Lorenzo retraced their tracks to find the other settlers who had stayed in Arizona. Not long into his trek, wolves began to trail him, waiting for him to die. He threw stones to scare them off, but they kept following. Without food or water, his quest seemed doomed, but members of the Pima nation found him wandering the desert and returned him to the settlers. The settlers took him in and sent a party out to try to find the missing Oatman sisters, but there was no trace of the girls. The search party buried the Oatmans as best they could in the hard desert ground where they had fallen. Alone now, Lorenzo eventually made his own way to California.

The modern marker at the site of the Oatman massacre.
Photo courtesy of Marine 69-71, CC 4.0.

Lorenzo probably thought he would never see his sisters again. In fact, that was true of Mary Ann. But five years later, Olive would reappear in California bearing the blue tattoos of the Mohave people on her face and arms. The settlers celebrated her return, but Olive spoke little of her time in captivity, and what she did say was contradictory. What actually happened to Olive during her desert survival story? And did she spend the rest of her life regretting that she'd ever come back?

When the Yavapai band attacked her family, Olive wasn't sure what was happening. She believed the people were Apaches, a group much feared for their attacks on white migrants. The Yavapai were normally peaceful, and at first, they were friendly with the Oatmans. Their attack seemed to come like a crash of thunder. We don't know why they killed the Oatmans. They may have been angry or desperate when Royce Oatman wouldn't share his family's meager supplies since the area was suffering a terrible famine that year. The discovery of another grave near the Oatmans' have led people to wonder if Royce attacked and killed one of the Yavapai first, or if the Yavapai had begun raiding other travelers during the famine.

Either way, Olive saw her father, mother, and brother Lorenzo struck down by clubs. She tried to help her family, but the Yavapai held her back and eventually hit her on the head to quiet her. She came to, expecting to die at any moment. Her sister Mary Ann was crying.

"Mother! O, mother! Olive, they are killed."

Olive heard groans from her dying mother and wanted to go back to her, but the Yavapai held her back.

"Please, kill me, too!" she said, but the Yavapai laughed at her.

The Yavapai had other plans. They marched the two Oatman girls back to their camp, stopping to eat the food they had stolen from the Oatmans. The Yavapai took most of their clothes and even their shoes, so Olive and Mary Ann left a trail of bloody footprints behind them. Olive and Mary Ann became slaves to the band, gathering seeds and firewood, hauling water, and doing other difficult and back-breaking chores. Their masters often beat them.

Then, a group of Mohave came to trade with the Yavapai. The daughter of the chief, a young woman named Topeka, was distressed to see two young girls treated so harshly, so she convinced her father to trade for the girls. With that, the Oatman girls seem to have fallen into better luck. They were adopted into the chief's family and were treated like sisters to Topeka. The Mohave gave them land to farm and Mohave names. Olive became Cloudwoman.

This map shows the Oatmans' route following the trail forged by the Mormon Battalion and the location of the Mohave village where Olive and Mary Ann eventually settled.

As part of adopting the girls into the tribe, the Mohave also tattooed the girls. Olive reported that the tattoos were made by pricking their skin with a very sharp stick and then rubbing dye from cactus juice and charcoal into their skin.

A Mohave girl with her face decorated or tattooed. Photo
Courtesy of the Library of Congress.

Olive would later say the tattoos marked them as slaves, but the Mohave didn't tattoo their slaves. The tattoos were meant to mark members of the tribe so they would recognize each other in the afterlife. If Olive understood this, then why did she lie? Some people have studied the pictures of the tattoos and said that they appear remarkable clean and clear, as if she had held still for the procedure instead of fighting it, such as trying to turn her head away. Maybe, thinking all of her family was gone, she was happy to be accepted into another family. Maybe she didn't have the strength to fight anymore.

Mary Ann died during a drought and famine in 1853, along with many other Mohave youth. The girls' adoptive mother Aespano howled in grief all night at Mary Ann's death. Olive was weak and sick, too, but Aespano sneaked her extra corn to save her life. The Mohave wanted to cremate Mary Ann, as was their custom, but Olive begged them to bury her instead, and the Mohave respected her wishes.

Olive may have thought she was alone in the world except her Mohave family. She didn't know that Lorenzo had survived, or that he was still hopeful of finding her. When white explorers came to the Mohave settlement, Olive kept herself hidden from them. She wasn't trying to be rescued.

A sketch of the Mohave village where Olive lived, drawn by a member of the expedition that passed through while she stayed with the Mohave.

Lorenzo had also lost all of his family, though, and he continued pestering everyone he could find to help him find what had happened to his sisters. Initially, the commander of Fort Yuma had refused to help, saying he didn't know if the massacre had occurred on the US or Mexican side of the border. Finally, a Yuma man named Francisco heard about Lorenzo's quest. He decided to find out what he could about the girls, and he learned that a white girl matching Olive's description was living with the Mohave.

When asked, the Mohave denied that Olive lived with them. They might have been afraid of being punished, or they might not have wanted to let Olive go once they had adopted her. But then Francisco returned with an order from the government to return the girl or explain why they couldn't. With the threat hanging over the tribe, Olive met with Francisco. She had become fluent in Mohave and had almost forgotten how to speak English, but she told him who she was. He also probably told her that her brother was alive.

Olive was in a terrible position. The Mohave were her family now, but the government was threatening them if she didn't return. And if she knew her brother was still alive, she also knew he had no one else. Olive agreed to return to Fort Yuma. Aespano wept at Olive's departure, and Olive cried on the long trip back to the fort. Lorenzo hurried to meet her there, and the two had a tearful reunion.

Fort Yuma on the Colorado River, where Olive traveled after leaving the Mohave village. Image courtesy of Wikimedia.

Everyone wanted to hear Olive's story, but she said little, only giving short answers when asked and struggling to remember English. Initially, she said she was eleven when her parents were killed, as though she were switching herself with Mary Ann. Maybe trauma had confused her mind. Maybe her life before the Mohave seemed like a strange dream she couldn't quite remember.

The two surviving Oatman siblings were together again, but their future did not look bright. They were orphans and only nineteen and twenty years old. The California government voted to raise money to help the brother and sister, but somehow the money never actually made it to them. A family who had traveled with the Oatmans before the massacre and later settled in California gave them a place to stay, and soon a distant cousin invited them to move to Oregon. Olive couldn't seem to settle down, though. She would stay up late at night, pacing the floors and weeping, presumably for the friends she had left behind.

Olive's appearance, and especially her facial tattoos, shocked nineteenth-century America. She struggled to adjust to life in white society. Photo courtesy of Wikimedia.

The siblings met a preacher named Royal B. Stratton who was fascinated by Olive's story and convinced her to let him write it. She agreed, and he spun a story that was melodramatic and probably half fiction, but it was a best seller. The money from the book allowed Lorenzo and Olive to go to college in California. But Olive would never be entirely comfortable. People gawked at her facial tattoos and considered her a freak, so she sometimes covered her face with a veil.

Stratton arranged for her to speak about her experiences, and many in the crowd treated it like a circus, coming to stare at the tattooed girl. It doesn't seem that she enjoyed the experience, but maybe she needed the money, or maybe she was trying to understand what her strange tale meant and who she was now.

In this photo of Olive, taken while she was touring the country, she wears a dress with designs that echo her tattoo. She was a skilled seamstress and might have created the dress herself. Was she trying to create an image that blended her Mohave and white American experiences? Photo courtesy of the National Portrait Gallery.

She toured the country telling her story—or, at least, telling stories. Some of the tales she told contradicted each other, as if she had trouble remembering or was just weaving stories for the audience and not to explain the truth. For instance, she had constantly said that the Mohave had treated her kindly, but many people at the time refused to believe that any Native Americans would be compassionate to a white captive, so she started to tell them that the Mohave had treated her as a slave. Stratton often "helped" her write her speeches, so maybe he was controlling the story she told.

It's hard to know for certain what Olive thought or remembered at that point, but when she heard that one of her Mohave friends, Chief Irataba, was nearby in Washington DC, she bought a train ticket to visit him. She wept with joy to see him and they spoke in Mohave. But it seemed she couldn't go back with him. Perhaps she felt that she couldn't leave her brother again, or maybe life in white society had become more comfortable for her.

Chief Irataba during his visit to Washington DC. Photo courtesy of Wikimedia.

While traveling, Olive met John B. Fairchild, a wealthy businessman, and they later married and settled in Texas. Rumors circulated that she had been married to a Mohave man and had left children behind, but she was never able to have children. She and Fairchild adopted an orphaned girl. Fairchild bought all the copies of Stratton's books that he could find and destroyed them. It's not clear if he did this because Olive was upset about the way Stratton had told her story, or if he was trying to put Olive's time with the Mohave in the past. Either way, once she was married, she never spoke of her time among the Mohave again, except sometimes in private letters with her brother and an aunt.

Olive suffered constant headaches and bouts of severe depression during her later life, but Fairchild was wealthy and provided her as comfortable a life as possible. She spent her time trying to help others, especially orphans. Clearly her time as a captive shaped her, but she kept the memories hidden beneath her veil along with her tattoos. Rumors circulated that she died in an insane asylum, but that was actually Stratton; Olive lived until age sixty-five, dying of a heart attack in 1903 at her Texas home. Even now, the full truth about her time among the Mohave remains a mystery.

THE OUTLAWS' HIDDEN LOOT

In 1871, an outlaw named John Reynolds lay low in a rough dugout cabin, hiding from the law and bleeding to death after getting shot while rustling cattle.

"It's no use," he said to his partner in crime, Albert Brown. "I'm going across the range soon."

Brown couldn't argue. He knew it was true. Cattle rustling was dangerous business, and not many outlaws lived to an old age.

"If only we could've made it back to Colorado," Reynolds said, his voice weak. "We wouldn't have needed to steal cattle." He coughed and struggled to draw another breath. "I've got $60,000 in cash and gold my brother and I buried in the mountains."

Brown had heard rumors about the Reynolds gang's loot, but this was straight from the horse's mouth. Unless Reynolds was delirious or telling tall tales.

Reynolds' face was pale. "Promise to bury me deep so the coyotes don't gnaw on my bones, and I'll tell you where it is."

"Done!" Brown said, his mouth dry with anticipation.

Reynolds described the location of the buried loot. Neither man had a pencil, so they mixed gunpowder with water to draw a map. When Reynolds died, Brown buried him as promised then headed north to claim his reward. But Brown never found it, and the outlaw's treasure may still be hidden in the mountains of Colorado.

The Reynolds Gang's home base in Colorado.

Colorado's history is sprinkled with gold and blood. Early European explorers reported rumors of gold, silver, and turquoise in Colorado, but nothing certain enough to trigger a gold rush. After the California Gold Rush of 1849, many miners who didn't strike it rich drifted to other parts of the West in hopes of finally hitting the bonanza. When a miner struck a rich vein of gold in Colorado in 1859, it brought a stampede of miners into the territory. As many as 10,000 people arrived in the first month alone, John and James Reynolds among them.

At the time, Colorado was part of the newly-formed Kansas Territory, known as "Bleeding Kansas" because of its violence. Congress allowed the territory to choose whether to allow slavery. Many of the miners who came with the gold rush, including the Reynolds brothers, came from Southern states and supported slavery, but others were abolitionists. This led to a prequel to the Civil War where pro- and anti-slavery forces burned, looted, and murdered each other.

By 1861, enough miners had settled in Colorado for the region to form its own territory. Just a few months later, the Civil War split the country into the Union in the North and the Confederacy in the South. The territories in the West had to choose sides. Texas joined the Confederacy. Kansas threw its lot in with the Union. Colorado also stayed with the Union—barely. But many Southern sympathizers like the Reynolds wanted to help the Confederacy in the West.

The Confederacy wanted their help, especially if it meant getting their hands on the riches coming out of the mines in Colorado and other Western states and territories. That money could help buy ammunition and supplies for the war.

Not only that, but the Confederacy wanted to disrupt communication between the US government in the East and the territories in the West. These lines of communication kept the Union together and brought news of the war West. Before telephones, radios, television, and the internet, that meant someone had to carry messages back and forth across hostile territory. Boats and stagecoaches took weeks or months to relay letters and news.

Starting in 1860, the boys of the Pony Express rode the mail across the country, making the trip in blistering heat and freezing cold, over vast prairies and steep mountains, and under threat of attack by Native Americans and

Confederate sympathizers—those who wanted the United States to lose. They did this all in only 10 days each way.

Telegraphs were an even faster method of communication used by both sides of the war, but they required a wire to carry the message. That meant that for the US government to send messages to the West, men had to walk across the entire length of the country setting up cables. Like the Pony Express riders, these men faced great dangers—and while a pony might outrace a wolf or bear, men on foot cannot—and the Confederacy was anxious to cut telegraph cables where it could. Nevertheless, the telegraph line was finished, connecting East and West for the Union and frustrating the Confederacy.

The Pony Express and telegraphs both helped the Union communicate with the West during the Civil War. Some Pony Express riders later carried messages for the Union Army and died in the line of duty. Image courtesy of the Library of Congress.

Still, the Confederates fought on in the West. The southern part of Arizona and New Mexico seceded from the Union and proclaimed themselves for the Confederacy. Confederate and Union forces fought a decisive battle at

Glorieta Pass in New Mexico, which stopped the Confederate's attempts to advance north and take out the Union forts. But that didn't stop Confederate soldiers from harassing Union forces.

Enter John and James Reynolds. They sympathized with the Confederacy's pro-slavery cause and, even more, they saw an opportunity to get richer off the war than they ever could mining. In 1861, they met up with a large encampment of Confederate sympathizers in Colorado at a place called Mace's Hole. The Union soldiers got word of the Confederate gathering and surprised the men there, arresting the Reynolds brothers with the others.

They were taken to jail in Denver and spent several months there until a sympathetic jailer helped them to escape. They fled to Texas to join the fight along with many other Colorado Confederates. Eventually, the Reynolds brothers gathered a "gang" of Confederates from Colorado and Texas under the command of the Third Texas Cavalry to harass Union forces in Colorado, and particularly to stop wagon trains and stagecoaches, interrupting the mail and stealing whatever gold and other resources they could get their hands on.

A stagecoach guarded by soldiers. Photo courtesy of Wikimedia.

In 1864, the Reynolds Gang plagued the Santa Fe Trail in southern Colorado, attacking Union forces and anyone else who crossed their path. They clashed with Native Americans and robbed a Mexican wagon train. The gang stole money meant to pay Union soldiers, gold from the mines, guns and ammunition, and the supplies they needed to keep raiding, certain they could soon gather and arm more recruits for the Confederacy, maybe even retake Colorado.

The coins, gold, and weapons weighed them down, so they set up a camp and visited local Confederates to gather information.

After learning more about the movement of the mail stagecoaches, James Reynolds announced, "I want to rob the coach when it reaches McLaughlin's ranch."

His brother and the rest of the men agreed, and they rode on to McLaughlin's, taking the rancher and his wife prisoner. When the stagecoach arrived at the ranch with two men on the drivers' seat, the Reynolds Gang surrounded them, guns drawn.

"Hands up!" James Reynolds ordered.

The driver Abe Williamson and the stage superintendent Billy McClellan obeyed. The gang surrounded the horses and took the two men's weapons.

"Climb down," James kept his pistol trained on the men. "And hand over your money."

"I'm just the driver," Williamson said. "I haven't got any!"

"Search them," James said with a flick of his pistol.

They searched McClellan's pockets and stole four hundred dollars and a gold watch. Williamson had only fifteen cents, which the bandits took. Williamson's face flushed red with embarrassment and anger.

There were no passengers, but the stagecoach was loaded with mail and a trunk for carrying valuables.

"Get the ax," James said.

"Don't break the trunk," McClellan said. "I have the key."

"We don't need a key." James sneered.

He smashed the trunk open, revealing its cargo of gold dust and refined gold from the Orphan Boy mine. His gang whooped in excitement.

"We're not done," James announced. "Check the mail."

His men pulled out knives and tore open letters, most of which were from miners sending news and money home to their families. The gang pocketed all the money they found.

"Destroy the stagecoach." James grinned. "Anything to hurt the US government."

His men hacked the coach to pieces.

"Now," James said, "McLaughlin's wife is going to make us a nice dinner, and our prisoners are going to stay here while we ride ahead and steal the extra stage horses at the Michigan Ranch." He pointed his gun at McClellan. "If you try to follow us, you die. There are 1,500 Texas Rangers coming to our aid, and 2,500 Confederate troops are marching north. They may be in Denver already."

James Reynolds may have thought his lie would terrify his prisoners into submission. Maybe he even thought it was half-true, since he planned to raise Confederate forces throughout the state. But he didn't count on McClellan's bravery or Williamson's anger.

As soon as the Reynolds Gang rode off, McClellan said, "We're under attack. I'm going to raise the alarm."

The others shook their heads. "They'll kill you."

"I have to try."

The marauders had stolen all the horses, but McClellan found a mule they'd left behind, and he rode night and day for the next week, warning all the nearby settlements and mining camps to be on the lookout for Confederate raiders. Some of those miners sympathized with the Confederacy, but they lost all sympathy when they learned the raiders had stolen the money they were sending home to their families. McClellan gathered a large enough posse of men that they might have stood a chance even against Reynolds' imaginary 4,000 men.

Meanwhile, the Reynolds Gang continued to plunder the countryside, stealing horses, food, and money. But everywhere they rode, scouts and posses were on the lookout for them. They sometimes exchanged gunfire, but the gang stayed on the run.

The Reynolds Gang's camp from Cook's book Hands Up.

They had far too much loot to carry with them, so James and John found an abandoned mine to hide the gold and cash. They wrapped the cash in silk cloth and put their treasure into cans in the mine. Then they blocked the entrance so no one would find it if they didn't know what they were looking for.

When they got back to camp, the gang talked about the possibility of splitting up and rendezvousing somewhere else later. James was dividing up the remaining gold dust among the men. A gunshot cracked in the mountain quiet. One of the men fell dead. Another boom, and a stinging pain seared James's arm. He dropped the can of gold dust as blood flowed down his arm.

One of the posses had found them.

The gang scattered for cover behind brush and boulders, but they were surrounded. The sun was setting, and the gang used the long shadows to try to slip away. Most did not make it far. The posse collected the can of gold dust, McClellan's watch, and all of the men except for John Reynolds and Jack Stowe, who was seriously wounded in the escape.

The posse hauled the gang to jail in Denver. There, General Cook tried to make James reveal the location of his loot.

"It's safe," James said.

When Cook pressed him further, James told him, "We sent it home."

"We'll send them to Fort Lyon and deal with them there," Cook said.

But the notoriously brutal Colonel Chivington of the Colorado cavalry had other plans. The soldiers he sent to escort them were men that the Reynolds gang had wronged or robbed, including stagecoach driver Abe Williamson.

"If they so much of think the word 'escape,' execute them," Chivington ordered. The men understood. The

Reynolds Gang had caused a heap of trouble, and they were not to reach Fort Lyon alive.

On the march, the soldiers gave the gang members plenty of chances to escape, which would be the excuse they needed to shoot them. The gang members knew better than to try. The soldiers finally decided to skip the formalities.

Williamson lined them up. "You're going to be shot. You violated civil and military law, and Chivington wants you executed."

James Reynolds raised his hands, which were heavy with the iron manacles chaining him. "Don't kill us. I once had you in my power and didn't harm you."

"Use what time you have left to make peace with your Maker," Williamson said.

The soldiers shot the marauders and left their bodies for the coyotes.

One of the men, John Andrews, passed out from his wound but didn't die. When he came to later to find the rest of his companions dead, he crawled to the house of a friend who nursed him back to health. Then, Andrews went south to New Mexico and rejoined John Reynolds and Jack Stowe, telling them what had become of the gang. They decided to go back for one of their caches of loot and continue the fight against the US forces in Colorado.

The three men stole horses from a Mexican ranch near Taos, and the ranchers pursued them, killing Stowe and Andrews. Only John Reynolds remained of the gang now.

The Civil War ended the next year, and Reynolds had chosen the wrong side. He didn't dare go back to Colorado to fetch the loot. He and his brother had been too well known there, and he didn't want to meet the same fate as James. On his own, John Reynolds changed his name and made a living as a gambler.

But gambling isn't a stable career choice, so John resorted to stealing when he needed to. That was how he ended up dying in a dugout cabin, leaving Albert Brown with the secret of the gang's loot.

Brown didn't know Colorado, so he enlisted the help of a local who had known the Reynolds Gang. They followed the map, but they quickly ran into a problem: a forest fire had swept through the area, destroying the trees that John Reynolds had used as landmarks. Floods and landslides are common after forest fires, further altering the landscape. The hidden mine with its lost loot could be anywhere. They searched until they ran out of supplies and returned empty-handed.

Without the treasure, Brown needed cash, so he robbed a stagecoach and stole some horses. It wasn't long before he was arrested and taken to jail in Denver—the same place where James Reynolds had refused to divulge the location of his stash of loot.

General Cook, who had questioned James, discovered that Brown had a map to the lost treasure. Somehow, he managed to get Brown's story—and the map. Perhaps that had something to do with how Brown escaped the jail in 1873. Brown was killed in a drunken fight not long after his escape.

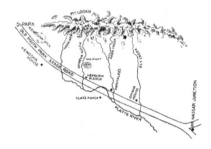

The Reynolds treasure map from Cook's book Hands Up.

Cook published a book with the story of the Reynolds Gang and the map. The map has excited treasure hunters ever since.

In 1906, a pair of miners did find a hidden trove of gold dust and old paper money, but it wasn't in the area that Reynolds had described it and it wasn't as much as Reynolds had promised. Perhaps they found only one stash of the Reynolds Gang's loot or even someone else's cache. Maybe Reynolds had remembered wrong where the loot lay hidden, or perhaps he had even lied. Whatever the case, the fortunes lost in Colorado during the Civil War may still be hidden somewhere in an old, covered mine shaft in the mountains.

7

THE LOST COMPANY OF THE LITTLE BIGHORN

In July of 1876, as the nation celebrated the 100th anniversary of the Declaration of Independence, news came that stopped many celebrations cold: Civil War hero George Armstrong Custer and all of the men under his direct command were dead, wiped out in a battle against the Sioux and Cheyenne at the Little Bighorn River in Montana territory.

The Army hastily buried Custer's men where they fell, hoping to return and study how it happened that an experienced commander lost several seasoned companies— over two hundred men. When they brought official military headstones to place on the field burials, the mystery deepened: an entire company of cavalrymen, Company E— the Gray Horse Company—was missing. To this day, their bodies have not been found, though many claim they haunt the battlefield; the neighboring Crow Nation residents call the rangers who care for the site "ghost herders."

This photograph from the Antietam Battlefield includes President Abraham Lincoln in the center with his famous top hat, while Custer lounges on the far right.

Even before his infamous death at the Little Bighorn, Custer had a colorful and questionable past. He joined West Point military academy in 1857, but he was a poor student—in fact, one of the worst in the academy's history. To make matters worse, he loved playing practical jokes. The academy considered expelling him.

In normal times, his military career might have ended before it even began, but in 1861, the Civil War splintered the nation. Nearly half of Custer's classmates dropped out of school to fight for the rebel Confederacy. West Point finished the rest of his class's training early to send them to fight for the Union. Custer graduated last in his class.

The Civil War gave Custer a chance to put his reckless energy to use, perhaps foreshadowing that fatal day awaiting him in Montana. Early in the war, Custer's cavalry unit under General McClellan chased a group of Confederate soldiers until the Union troops encountered the Chickahominy River in Virginia. The senior officers hesitated, trying to decide how best to cross to swift, dangerous waters.

"I wish I knew how deep it is," one of the generals said.

Custer took that as his cue. He charged into the racing river in front of the startled officers.

"That's how deep it is, General," he called.

An illustration of Custer charging into the Chickahominy. Some accounts say he was on horseback instead of on foot. Courtesy of the Library of Congress.

McClellan was impressed by Custer's daring and allowed him to lead a group of soldiers in the attack. The Union won the fight, and Custer began his up-and-down career, being promoted and demoted several times. At one point, Custer was literally up and down: his commanders assigned him to use a hot air balloon to scout enemy positions—one of the first Americans to engage in aerial warfare.

One of the Union's Civil War hot air balloons. Photo courtesy of the Library of Congress.

His long blond hair and the flashy way he dressed up his uniform stood out among his fellow officers. He gained a reputation for being lucky; he survived having eleven horses shot and killed under him, only getting one minor injury during the entire war.

The Battle of Gettysburg was the turning point of the Civil War, and Custer played his part. His cavalry unit, though badly outnumbered, charged against the Confederate cavalry. The impact of the men and horses clashing sent many horses tumbling over and crushing their riders.

"I challenge the annals of warfare to produce a more brilliant or successful charge of cavalry," Custer later said.

Custer's daring charge helped to break up the Confederate cavalry and secure the Union victory. Custer also lost more men at Gettysburg than any other Union cavalry commander.

Custer came out of the war a hero and decided to stay with the cavalry. That meant going West. More settlers were anxious to move into lands traditionally occupied by Native Americans, and Native Americans sometimes retaliated by attacking travelers or settlements. The settlers looked to the Army to protect them.

But, after his heroic actions in the Civil War, Custer's behavior in the West had some military commanders questioning if he was fit to lead. He shot deserters without a fair trial, and he once went AWOL (absent without leave). The Army court-martialed him for his actions and suspended him without pay.

To some, Custer seemed too headstrong and unreliable to remain in the Army, but others in command sympathized with his reasons for acting as he did. When fighting broke out with the Cheyenne, the Army called Custer back to the 7th Cavalry, and he would be an "Indian Fighter" until the fateful day at Little Bighorn eight years later. Did his rashness and willingness to act against orders lead directly to his last stand?

Conflict with the Cheyenne and Sioux intensified when gold was discovered on their lands in the Black Hills of South Dakota—during an expedition led by Custer. The Black Hills were sacred to both the Cheyenne and the Sioux people, and the US government had signed a treaty promising the Black Hills to the Sioux, but in the gold rush that followed, the government backed out of their agreement and tried to move the Sioux to a different reservation.

Lakota Sioux religious and military leader Sitting Bull, who organized resistance against the US Army. Photo courtesy of Wikimedia.

The broken treaty angered the Sioux. Many refused to return to the reservations or, because of their nomadic lifestyle, didn't even know about the government's demand. Instead, they gathered in the Montana territory where they joined with Arapaho and Cheyenne under the leadership of religious leader Sitting Bull and warrior Crazy Horse.

The army sent Custer with about 500 men as one part of a three-pronged mission to bring the various tribes back to the reservations. He was aided by scouts and warriors of the Crow and Arikara people, who were traditional enemies of the Sioux. Custer was supposed to find the main Sioux-Cheyenne encampment and wait, hidden, on one side until the other two Army detachments arrived so they would have the Native camp surrounded. Then they would attack together.

The location of the Battle of Little Bighorn.

As the cavalry commanders parted ways for their mission, one of the other officers said, "Now Custer, don't be greedy. Wait for us."

"I won't," Custer said.

The other commanders must have hoped that Custer meant he wouldn't be greedy for action and rush into the fight, but they couldn't be sure the daredevil commander didn't mean, "I won't wait."

By mid-June of 1876, Custer's detachment had come near the Little Bighorn River, where the Sioux and Cheyenne had their main encampment. The summer sun pounded the prairie, sucking the green from the landscape and sending the rattlesnakes looking for shade. The cavalry horses kicked up a trail of dust along the trail, and sweat ran down the soldiers' backs and made their blue wool uniforms itch.

The scouts reported the encampment on the river to Custer but warned him that the soldiers wouldn't be able to sneak up on it during the daytime.

Custer didn't want the Sioux and Cheyenne to see the soldiers coming and move their encampment somewhere else. He decided to try to get closer to the village by marching in the dark of the night of the 24th. The moon was only a sliver in the sky, and the men rode with the stars bright overhead and the wind blowing through the long grass and sagebrush of the plains.

Custer with his Arikara and Crow scouts. Some would die with him on the battlefield. Photo courtesy of Wikimedia.

By morning, Custer's scouts arrived with bad news: the encampment had likely seen the cavalry's approach.

"There's no chance now to surprise them," Custer told his subordinates, Major Reno and Colonel Benteen. "We divide into three columns and attack."

Custer was acting against orders, but he didn't want the warriors to escape. He took 210 soldiers with him, left about 140 with Reno, and had Benteen in the rear with 125 soldiers and the extra supplies and ammunition. Without specific orders, Reno and Benteen marched forward.

Company E—the Gray Horse Company—rode on with Custer and four other companies, confident they could defeat the Native warriors. What Custer and his soldiers didn't know was the massive size of the encampment. They thought it was a small hunting party, not the 8,000 or so men, women, and children gathered together, which included over 1,500 warriors compared to about 500 soldiers under Custer. Not only that, but the Native warriors were better armed. Some still used bows and arrows or old muzzle-loading guns, but many had taken single shot rifles in fights with cavalry soldiers, and others had six-shooter pistols and repeating rifles that could shoot more quickly than the cavalry guns.

Imagine how the cavalry soldiers felt as they rode toward the river through the hills and ravines dotted with sagebrush. They had been riding all night, and the sun beat down on them and sapped their energy. Their horses' reins jangled as the tired animals shook their heads and swished tails to shoo the flies buzzing around them. The odor of dust and horse droppings filled their noses. The soldiers knew they were supposed to wait for the other cavalry units, but their commander was anxious for a fight. Some of them might have been excited, too, and probably nervous. They couldn't know that many of them had seen their last sunrise.

A messenger from Custer brought word to Reno: "The village is only two miles ahead and running away. Move forward as fast as you can and then charge. The whole outfit will support you."

Reno and his soldiers charged down the ravine to the river where the encampment was located. They were not prepared for the number or the ferocity of the resistance they met. After all, this was not a small hunting band—it was a village of families, with men ready to fight to protect their wives, mothers, sisters, and young sons and brothers.

A Sioux warrior, Little Soldier, later said, "Bullets sounded like hail on tepees and tree tops."

Reno and his surviving soldiers retreated under the fire of Native guns and arrows and fled back up the ravine. There, they fell in with Benteen's unit.

Custer had sent a soldier back to Benteen with a written message.

Come on. Big Village. Be Quick. Bring Packs. P.S. Bring Packs.

The messenger, Sergeant Charles Windolph, said that his last view of Custer was of the commander and his soldiers galloping into a ravine, the Grey Horse Company in the center.

Benteen couldn't follow Custer, though. Sioux and Cheyenne warriors swarmed up the ravines after Reno's soldiers. Reno and Benteen found a sagebrush-covered ridge above the river that offered some protection from the arrows and bullets. Their soldiers quickly dug a shallow ridge and breastwork to hold out against the warriors circling them.

Benteen attempted to send reinforcements to Custer. The soldiers reached a rise now called Weir Point where they could see the distant fighting, but the Native warriors pushed them back.

Reno and Benteen's companies were pinned down, unable to help Custer and unable to flee. The sun beat down on them and dust rose to coat their throats and noses. Wounded soldiers groaned in pain and cried out for a drink to sooth their parched mouths. A few brave soldiers sneaked down a ravine to the river under heavy Native fire to bring water back. The next afternoon, Reno and Benteen's surviving soldiers were relieved to see the Sioux retreat and Army reinforcements coming to their rescue. They had heard nothing from Custer and hoped that he had somehow survived the fighting.

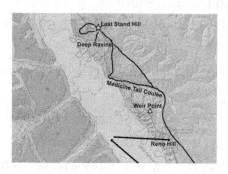

A map showing Reno's attack and retreat (dark arrows),
Benteen's path (light arrow), and the route likely taken by
Custer's forces to Last Stand Hill.

They found Custer and all the soldiers who had ridden out with him dead. It appeared that the last of Custer's soldiers had shot their horses and used their bodies in an attempt to create a breastwork on the rise known as Last Stand Hill, as Reno's soldiers had done with the dirt and sagebrush. Custer had been shot once in the chest and once in the temple.

The victorious warriors had withdrawn, so the only immediate clues about what happened at Custer's Last Stand were those left on the battlefield—bodies and bullet casings. Later, some of the warriors told their stories, but many did not want to speak up for fear of retribution, and white historians didn't always believe them. Over time, stories and memories fade, and some of the accounts from the Sioux and Cheyenne don't agree about details of the battle.

A painted buffalo hide based on the Cheyenne memory of the battle. Photo courtesy of izanbar via Deposit Photos.

The evidence shows that Custer divided his forces, sending some of them down Medicine Tail Coulee (a coulee is a steep ravine leading down to the river). At this point, Custer already knew he was outnumbered, so why divide his forces further? Some people have speculated that he was hoping to help or rally Reno, as he did not know that Reno's charge had already failed. Others have speculated that he was trying to divide the Sioux-Cheyenne forces by feigning an attack on the village where the women and children were, drawing warriors back to protect the village.

Whatever Custer was planning, there is only a little evidence of fighting in the coulee, as if the soldiers scrambled down to the river, then turned around and went back up without any clear cause. Perhaps they saw that Reno wasn't there and the Native women and children had already retreated to safety. Perhaps they knew that their comrades on the ridge above needed help.

But Custer's troops were never able to reunite. The evidence of bullet casings and fallen soldiers show that many of his soldiers died huddled in small groups, probably trying to defend themselves. Today, the line of tombstones on the battlefield points north, showing the desperate struggle of soldiers to catch up with their commander, where he raced toward his final moments on Last Stand Hill with the remainder of his soldiers, including the Gray Horse Company.

In fact, many bullet casings have been found past Last Stand Hill, as if Custer or some of his soldiers rode on and then turned back for the hill. Was Custer trying to escape with whatever of his men remained? Was he trying to find a way to the river in a desperate attempt to meet up with Reno and Benteen, who would never be coming to his aid?

Either way, the warriors drove Custer and his soldiers back to the high point of Last Stand Hill, a rallying point for any of his troops who remained.

Oglala Sioux Foolish Elk said, "When the horses got to the top of the ridge the gray ones and bays became mingled, and the soldiers with them were all in confusion."

Headstones on Last Stand Hill looking down toward the ravines leading to the river. Native warriors used the ravines as cover to attack the soldiers. Photo courtesy of DonyaNedomam via Deposit Photos.

That meant that the Gray Horse Company was with Custer at that point, though the soldiers were probably panicked. Custer had about 100 of his soldiers—a little less than half of his original force. Sniper fire pinned them in place, and the warriors scattered many of their horses, making it harder to escape, but the soldiers still had their weapons.

Warrior accounts tell us that a group of men broke away from the last stand and charged for one of the ravines. This is generally believed to be the lost company—the Gray Horse Company. The body of their commander, Lieutenant Smith, was found near Custer, but the rest of the company were never located.

We don't know why they broke away. If they were panicking, it's strange that they did it as an organized unit. If they were trying to run for help, why charge down the ravine toward the Native village—and right into their attackers? Was it meant to be a heroic last charge, or did Custer entrust them with some mission, like a final attempt to find Reno and Benteen or to stop the snipers firing at them from the ravine? If so, Lieutenant Smith must have already been injured or dead, or else why wouldn't he have led his own soldiers?

There are other questions about Custer's Last Stand. Why didn't he try to go south where he might meet up with Reno and Benteen? Why did he stay so long on that high point, just waiting, it seems? This was the daredevil of West Point, after all.

With the loss of the Gray Horse Company, Custer's numbers were once again cut nearly in half, and Custer faced his last moments. And that brings up the last question: who killed Custer?

No warrior admitted to being the one who shot Custer. Custer had been known for his long, blond hair, but he had cut it short for the battle, so many of the warriors would not have recognized him, making it harder to determine what happened in Custer's last moments.

We now know that shortly before the day of the battle, a group of young warriors had made a pact that in their next battle they would either kill their enemies or die in battle. This group of young warriors fought on the north end of the battle, against Custer and his soldiers. It may be that they were the ones who faced Custer.

There have also been some suggestions that Custer and the last of his soldiers shot themselves or each other rather than allow themselves to be taken prisoner. Foolish Elk reporting seeing one soldier fleeing on horseback and then shooting himself when several warriors pursued him. The soldiers might have been afraid of being tortured as prisoners or used in bargaining against the US Government, or they might, like the young warriors, have decided they would die on the battlefield.

The warriors took weapons, money, and even the clothes of some of the soldiers. Though they certainly used some of the silver and other things they stole, there were rumors that some of this battlefield loot is still buried out there in the harsh plains of Montana.

The bodies of the Gray Horse Company are lost out there somewhere, too. A fire in 1983 burned away the thick sagebrush covering the battlefield, allowing archaeologists to do an in-depth study of the site. They confirmed that the markers on the field corresponded with soldiers' bodies and uncovered trails of bullets that helped to tell the story of the battle. But they still didn't find the bodies of the missing soldiers of the Gray Horse Company. Many believe they must be in Deep Ravine, buried under soil eroded over the last century, but so far, no one has found a trace of them.

The prairie keeps it secrets.

8

THE MURDER OF DI LEE OF DEADWOOD GULCH

All old mining towns had their violent side, and they probably have their ghost stories, too, but Deadwood, South Dakota, is supposedly haunted by the ghost of the most beautiful woman in the West: Di Lee. Her death was as mysterious as her life, a murder that was never solved, and people say they still hear her phantom voice crying, "Don't kill me!"

Custer's discovery of gold in the Black Hills brought a stampede of prospectors to South Dakota. A settlement called Deadwood Gulch sprang to life almost overnight.

Deadwood in the Black Hills on the border of South Dakota.

Deadwood was formed of various mining camps packed into the narrow gulch named for the fallen trees found there. By 1877, Deadwood was a boom town in full swing, including a Chinese neighborhood along Main Street known as the Badlands.

Deadwood today, tucked into the gulch. Photo courtesy of YAYImages via Deposit Photos.

Like many immigrants to the West, most of the Chinese first came looking for gold, though they faced severe racism and sometimes violence from other miners. Chinese miners were among the Forty-Niners who headed to California for the Gold Rush. After the Civil War, it was predominantly Chinese workers who built the western portion of the great Transcontinental Railroad that united the country. Many Chinese workers continued east, chasing the gold fields with other miners.

Women were rare in mining boom towns, and the miners missed them. Some men would have liked to find a pretty girl to marry, but they also weren't used to doing their own cooking and laundry—jobs usually taken by women. Some of the Chinese miners saw an opportunity there. Panning for gold made a few people rich, but it left many others broke.

Yet the people who provided food, supplies, and services like laundry to the miners always managed to make a decent living. So, Deadwood's China town soon offered restaurants, laundries, and hotels for hungry, dusty miners fresh from panning for gold.

Chinese miners panning for gold. Image courtesy of Wikimedia.

Deadwood did draw a few women, and the most famous and mysterious of these was Di Lee. She was one of few Chinese women in the United States at the time, but she wasn't there to cook or do laundry. She was rich—rich enough to come into town and buy up several buildings. No one knew where she had come from or how she got her money. Many believed she came from San Francisco. Rumors said that she had been a servant or slave in California but had escaped and taken her master's money with her. What everyone did know was that she was single, independent, and very attractive. She came to be known as the China Doll for her remarkable beauty.

Some of the Chinese immigrants in Deadwood made money selling opium. Opium was a drug that was popular in

China and mainly used by Chinese customers, though the Chinese-owned shops catered to White and Black customers as well. Opium wasn't yet illegal, but many people worried about its effects. It was highly addictive and caused slower reactions and thinking, and sometimes even death.

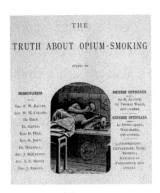

One of many books warning against opium use. Image courtesy of Wikimedia.

Di Lee was one of those who disliked opium. Perhaps she'd had a bad experience with it, didn't like the way it made people act slow and stupid, or had seen someone die from opium. Regardless of the reason, she spoke out against opium, saying it should be banned. This made some of the other Chinese residents angry at her, but it didn't stop her from speaking her mind.

On November 27, 1877, Di Lee answered a knock on the door. Someone hit her in the face with the handle of an ax. Another person knifed her in the chest.

"Don't kill me!" Di Lee called in Cantonese—her last words.

Even in a mining town like Deadwood, where fists fights

and even gun battles weren't uncommon, the murder of Di Lee shocked the community—the Chinese community especially.

Police suggested that three people were involved: one kept watch while the other two attacked her. The murder was baffling because it didn't appear that she had been robbed. The opium den owners seemed the most likely suspects, attacking her in revenge for speaking out against their business. It was also possible that her secret past had caught up with her—if she had stolen her money from a former master, he might have hunted her down. Or maybe, one of the residents of Deadwood was jealous of a rich property owner who was Chinese and a woman.

The Chinese community buried her in secret, and the location of her grave is still unknown. Did someone have something to hide, or were they trying to protect Di Lee's body from her enemies?

The police suspected a Chinese man named Ah Sing and his wife knew something about the murder. They arrested the couple, but the husband and wife admitted nothing, and no one would testify against them. Were they innocent? Or were people too afraid to speak up against them after the murder of Di Lee? The local newspaper reported that a Chinese girl took refuge in a hotel from several angry Chinese men because she said she knew who killed Di Lee, but the police didn't believe the story—or were too afraid to find out what the girl knew.

After Di Lee's death, a man named Hong Lee showed up and claimed to be her relative. The Deadwood coroner turned over Di Lee's property to him. We don't know if or how he was related to her. Maybe he just hoped to profit by the death of someone with the same common last name. Maybe he even had something to do with her murder.

If Hong Lee had hoped to make money by renting out Di Lee's buildings, he would be disappointed. Someone did move into the building not long after her death. Their first night in the new house, they thought they heard someone knocking at the door.

"Let me in," a male voice called.

The door creaked, and the new residents heard the sound of a struggle. They ran downstairs, but the door was still locked and the room was empty and still.

The neighbors reported hearing the struggle as well, followed by a woman calling, "Moo shoot nghin"—Cantonese for, "Don't kill me."

Di Lee's last words.

Convinced that the house was haunted, the new residents didn't stay another night. No one else would live there, either. Local residents believed that Di Lee haunted the building, angry that no one had spoken out and helped solve her murder.

Deadwood didn't forget Di Lee. They remembered her in later years in Deadwood's annual Days of '76 Parade, when a beautiful young girl was chosen to represent her each year on one of the parade floats. And perhaps Di Lee's ghost still lingers in Deadwood today, because no one ever confessed what they knew about the murder of Deadwood's China Doll.

9

THE CURSED TREASURE OF THE SUPERSTITION MOUNTAINS

Would you risk your life for a treasure that might be cursed?

For hundreds of years, that's just what people have done in the Superstition Mountains of Arizona. Many people have gone into the mountains searching for lost gold, and many never returned.

The harsh climate of the mountains likely caused some of the deaths and disappearances. Located in the Sonora Desert, where temperatures in the summer often exceed 110 degrees Fahrenheit, there's little water in the Superstitions except when flash floods crash through canyons and wash away everything in their path. Food is scarce, the cliffs are steep and rugged, and thorny plants and poisonous snakes and scorpions add to the danger.

But there may be more to the Superstitions than the brutal desert climate. For as long as people have gone there looking for lost treasure, others have claimed that the mountains are cursed.

The Superstitions, located in the desert near Phoenix.

Ancient cliff dwellings found near the Superstitions prove that people once lived in this area, probably the Salado and Hohokam cultures that mysteriously abandoned their homes around 1450. The Pima people, who are likely descended from the Hohokam, say that an evil spirit lives in the Superstition Mountains and kills people who venture too close. The Apache, who later made their homes nearby, believe that a god lives there who punishes trespassers.

But the Spanish who came to the Southwest in the 1500s seeking gold disregarded these warnings because they had also heard stories about treasure in the Superstition Mountains. According to legend, the Spanish who ventured out to find gold never returned.

Later stories from the 1800s claim that a Mexican family named Peralta found gold in the Superstition Mountains. The stories say they mined in secret for a while, but when the US won Arizona from Mexico in the Mexican-American War in 1848, the Peraltas tried to escape to Mexico with the gold. A group of Apaches caught them and shot all except two young boys.

There is much confusion about exactly who the Peraltas were, but the story of their mine ties into a man whom we know more about, and who would make the Superstition gold famous: Jacob Waltz.

Waltz was a German immigrant who'd traveled the country prospecting, but people always got to the good claims before he did. He finally settled in Arizona near Phoenix, not far from the Superstitions. Government records show that he filed two mining claims in the area, though there's no evidence he found anything significant at either site.

This is where history blurs into legend. Some stories claim that Waltz saved the life of one of the Peralta boys who had returned to find the abandoned mine. In gratitude, the young man told him where to find the treasure. Another story claims Waltz came across the Peralta boys mining their old claim and killed them to steal their gold. Others say the Peraltas never existed and Waltz found the mine on his own. But all the stories agree that Jacob Waltz had a secret source of gold.

Gold is often found with other minerals. Photo courtesy of Fireflyphoto via Deposit Photos.

Even the existence of gold in the Superstition Mountains raises questions. The mountains are the product of ancient volcanoes, which are not usually good places to find gold. Some geologists theorize that gold could exist in the mountains if natural forces pushed the minerals up from deeper beneath the earth.

Another theory is that the gold came from somewhere else and was hidden in the mountains—by Aztecs fleeing the Spanish conquistadors in the 1500s, by Apaches protecting their lands from outsiders, or by Mexicans fleeing the Mexican-American War. Or that Waltz found the gold somewhere else and hid it in the mountains so people wouldn't steal it or kill him for it.

Whether it was from a mine or a cache of lost treasure, Waltz sometimes showed up in town with gold ore to sell, though he was quiet about where it came from.

Then, in 1891, a flash flood destroyed Waltz's home, and he became ill from pneumonia contracted during the flood. His neighbor, a mixed-race woman named Julia Thomas, took him in and cared for him, but he was getting old and knew that the infection would kill him. As he grew weaker, he told Julia where she could find his mine.

The grave of Jacob Waltz. Photo courtesy of Marine 69-71,
CC 3.0.

After Waltz died, Julia and her neighbors found a box of gold ore with his possessions.

People have since doubted the existence of Waltz's mine, but Julia believed in it enough to bet everything she owned on it. She organized an expedition along with her two neighbors who had seen the ore, using everything she had to pay for the trip. Unfortunately for her, she came back empty-handed. A year later, gold was discovered just west of the Superstitions, along the route Waltz had drawn for Julia, but it wasn't Waltz's lost mine, and Julia had lost everything.

Julia needed a way to survive and recover from her financial losses. She decided to sell copies of her map to the "Lost Dutchman's Mine." Dutchman was another way of saying Deutsch-man, or German. She recouped her money, and the search for the mine has been ongoing since then. With it have come the disappearances and murders.

The Sonora Desert can be a deadly place. Photo courtesy of jomo333 via Deposit Photos.

In 1931, a veterinarian named Dr. Adolph Ruth showed up in Arizona with an old treasure map his son had found in Mexico—maybe a copy of Julia's map. Ruth convinced a pair of locals to guide him to a site in the Superstition Mountains, where he set up camp, determined to follow the map to a lost gold mine. When no one at the nearby ranch heard from him for a while, they went to check on him, but his campsite was deserted. Searchers looked for weeks but found no trace of Ruth. He had vanished.

Then, six months later, the deputy sheriff and the rancher found a skull. Dental records proved it was Ruth. The skull appeared to have a bullet wound.

"Maybe he shot himself," some said.

But the next month, they found the rest of Ruth's body elsewhere along with his gun. No bullets had been fired. In his checkbook was a note in Ruth's handwriting claiming that he had found the famed Lost Dutchman's Mine.

Ruth's last written words were *veni, vidi, vici,* a Latin phrase meaning, "I came, I saw, I conquered."

It didn't seem that anything of his had been stolen, including the map. No one knew who had killed him, or why. Adolph Ruth became one of a series of strange deaths in the Superstition Mountains related to the Lost Dutchman's Mine.

Coyotes in the Superstitions could have moved the bones of people who were killed or went missing searching for the treasure. Photo courtesy of cybernesco via Deposit Photos.

Before Ruth, in 1910, a woman's skeleton had been found in a cave in the Superstition Mountains surrounded by several gold nuggets. No one ever discovered who she was or how she died in a cave with the gold.

In 1945, writer and explorer Barry Storm wrote *Thunder God's Gold* about his adventures searching for the Lost Dutchman's treasure. He claimed that a mysterious sniper had shot at him in the Superstition Mountains. He speculated that it was the same person who shot Adolph Ruth.

The mysterious injuries and deaths continued. Some people said rocks fell on them as if pushed from above. Bodies were found without heads, and skulls without bodies. Several men went looking for the gold and were later found shot: Dr. John Burns in 1951, Joseph Kelley in 1952, and Hilmer Charles Bowen in 1961 to name a few. In each case, the deaths were ruled accidental and there was no hint of the killer.

Others simply disappeared.

Perhaps the strangest disappearance was in 1958. A campsite was found abandoned in the Superstition Mountains. The campsite contained a bloodied blanket, a Geiger counter for checking radiation levels, and equipment for cleaning a gun—though the gun was missing. There were also several letters and papers scattered throughout the campsite—but all the names and addresses had been carefully torn away to disguise the identity of the missing person. To this day, the identity and the fate of the victim remain a mystery.

Modern technology gives us new ways to look at old

problems. The gold nuggets Waltz had when he died have been passed down through private collectors, and scientists have analyzed their chemistry, comparing them to gold found in other places. But the nuggets are unique. They don't match gold mined from anywhere else, and only one matching sample has ever been found—by a man who died just after claiming to have proof that he found the mine.

That man was Walt Gassler. As a young man, he met the rancher who tried to help Adolph Ruth.

"I didn't want a bunch of tourists tromping on my land and spooking my cattle," the old rancher told Gassler. "But I think that mine is out there."

The treasure-hunting bug sunk its teeth into Gassler, and he spent over fifty years studying and searching for the Lost Dutchman's Mine.

The Weaver's Needle is supposed to be a landmark on the trail to the Lost Dutchman Mine. Photo courtesy of Chris C. Jones, CC 2.5

In 1984, the Superstition Mountains were set to be designated as a protected wilderness area, which meant mining would no longer be allowed there. But 82-year-old

Gassler said he had discovered the mine. He provided a sample of the gold ore he had found and copies of all of his research to a friend, Tom Kollenborn, who was a historian. Hoping to have a TV show made about his discovery, he returned to the mountains to bring back more proof. He had asked two friends to come along, including Kollenborn, but they couldn't go for a couple of days, and Gassler decided to go alone. His body was found five days later.

Gassler's death was ruled as natural causes—possibly a heart attack—but there were several strange things about it. Some people reported seeing armed men in the area at about the time his body was found. Bruises suggested that he had either been hit in the face or had fallen on his side, but he was found sitting up. And his backpack, found with his body, contained more gold nuggets, but later disappeared. Yet if someone ambushed the elderly Gassler, why wouldn't they have stolen the backpack, or at least taken the gold?

Soon after, someone claiming to be Gassler's son Roland showed up to talk to Kollenborn.

The man showed Kollenborn a piece of gold ore, which looked like the ones Gassler had produced, and said, "I know my dad found the mine, and I want to prove it. Can you give me a copy of the map he left with you?"

"I don't have the map anymore," Kollenborn told him, "but I have a copy of his manuscript."

The young man thanked him and took the papers detailing Gassler's search for the mine.

Not long after, another man approached Kollenborn and introduced himself as Roland Gassler.

"You're not Roland," Kollenborn said. "I've met him."

The young man looked flabbergasted. "But, I am Roland Gassler."

"Let's see some proof."

The young man pulled out his driver's license, which showed that he was the real Roland Gassler.

The mystery man who claimed to be Gassler's son had some of Gassler's ore, so maybe he was the one who stole the backpack. Unless he comes forward, we'll probably never know how he got the ore or if he ever found more of it.

Walt Gassler may have found the Lost Dutchman Mine—if it even exists—and he may have been killed to keep his knowledge a secret. And perhaps he wasn't the first. The mystery skeleton woman, Dr. Adolph Ruth, and many of the others found dead over the years also may have found the mine or gotten too close to its secrets. But who has been protecting the mine or the gold cache for all these years? Ancient spirits? Jealous rival miners? Locals who don't like tourists? We may never know.

THE LYNCHING OF CATTLE KATE

In July of 1889, the careers of the notorious Wyoming cattle rustler Cattle Kate and her sniveling, murderous boyfriend Jim Averell finally came to an end with an act of vigilante justice. Wyoming ranchers, sick of the couple's crimes, caught and lynched the thieving pair, and frontier justice was served. Their bodies were left hanging for days while newspapers celebrated the death of Cattle Kate, and the murder investigation against the ranchers was tossed out.

There was a problem with this story, though: Cattle Kate was a fictional character. The real-life woman whose body was left swinging in the sun was homesteader and cook Ella Watson, and Jim Averell was the local postmaster and a justice of the peace. So, what led a group of ranchers to hang a cook and a postmaster, and how did they get away with murder?

In early 1889, tales of Cattle Kate spiced up newspapers from California to New York. The stories claimed that Kate

Maxwell was a beautiful actress from Chicago who moved to Wyoming with her husband to start a cattle ranch. She brought her racehorses with her, and they could outrun any horse in the territory. She liked to watch her favorite bulldog fight wolves and coyotes, and it always won.

The completion of the Transcontinental Railroad in 1869 made Wyoming ranching a profitable business: ranchers could raise the cattle for free on public land in the West and then ship them to meat-hungry markets in the East. These "cattle barons" made fortunes on the range. Sensational newspaper stories said Kate wanted the cattle business for herself, so she poisoned her husband and took over the ranch, becoming Cattle Queen Kate.

One evening, as the tale goes, Kate returned from racing her fastest thoroughbred horse across the range to find that her ranch hands had taken 1500 dollars from her.

"They ain't getting away with that!" she said as she grabbed her pistols.

She jumped straight onto her thoroughbred and raced to the saloon in nearby Bessemer just as it was getting dark. As she suspected, her ranch hands were there, gambling with her money. She kicked the door open and stormed in, guns drawn. Before anyone could react, she shot the hat off one of the men.

Her ranch hands jumped to their feet. "We're sorry we took the money, Kate. We would have won it back by now, plus more, but these fellows are cheating."

Kate picked up the hat she had shot off the man's head, and sure enough, he had extra cards hidden there.

The saloon owner held up his hands. "Look, we'll give you back your money. No harm done."

Kate held out her gun. "You're right about one thing. You'll give me back my money."

The saloon owner did, then Kate nodded to her ranch hands. They grabbed the rest of the money on the card table and ran. As they escaped, Kate turned and shot her pistol into a burning oil lamp. The hot oil splattered, catching the saloon on fire. As men shouted and stampeded around the room trying to put out the flames, Kate sauntered out of the saloon, a smile on her lips, money in her pocket, and her pistol in her hand. The fire from the burning building lit her path back to the ranch for some distance.

A Wyoming newspaper, the Casper Weekly Mail, responded to the Cattle Kate stories in March of 1889, "It is a fine tale of western life, and is 'correct, with one exception.' That exception being the fact that not one word of it is true. There never existed in this part of Wyoming any such personage as 'Cattle Kate,' nor was there ever a saloon in Bessemer."

The Cattle Kate stories originated in Cheyenne, Wyoming in early 1889, but it's unclear who wrote them and sent them by telegraph to newspapers all over the country. If local newspaper men of the day knew, they weren't naming names. Maybe it was a hopeful writer who wanted to make a name for him or herself, or someone who wanted to make Wyoming sound like a wild and exciting place to live.

For a more truthful account of Western life, and especially the lives of women, we can turn to the life of the real "Cattle Kate," Ella Watson.

The real Ella Watson shows little resemblance to the stories
of "Cattle Kate." Photo courtesy of Wikimedia.

Ella was born in Canada, but when she was a girl, her family moved to Kansas to claim a homestead. The Homestead Act of 1862 said that anyone who moved west and improved a 160-acre plat of public land, meaning they built a house and supported themselves there for five years, could claim the land as a homestead for a ten-dollar fee. This brought stampedes of people west. But it wasn't an easy life. Homesteaders had to work hard and be self-reliant, since neighbors and towns were often miles away and roads and trains were unavailable or unreliable.

Ella developed a knack for cooking, and when she turned eighteen in 1879, she found a job in a town away from the family homestead. She was tall and full-figured with a pretty face but certainly not an actress, working as a cook and housekeeper at a hotel or boarding house. While there, she caught the attention of farm worker William

Pickle. He was charming enough to convince Ella to marry him.

After the wedding, things quickly changed.

In the 1800s, once a woman married, she lost many of her rights. Most women couldn't vote anyway, and married women also couldn't own property in many states or even keep the money they earned at their jobs—everything went to their husbands. Pickle started taking all of Ella's money and using it to get drunk. Sometimes, he would hit her. Ella couldn't go to anyone for help. Most people would say a husband could do what he wanted with his wife.

One night, Pickle had been drinking and got especially ugly. He pulled out a horse whip and lashed Ella with it. Ella wasn't a tiny woman, but Pickle was strong, and Ella couldn't stop him. She could escape, though. As soon as she had the chance, she ran back to her parents' house and did something very scandalous for the time: she filed for a divorce.

Ella still needed to get far away from William Pickle, but being divorced gave her options. For one thing, a married woman couldn't claim a homestead, but a single, divorced, or widowed woman could. That didn't mean it was considered normal or proper, though. Ella must have had an adventurous or rebellious streak, because she moved on her own to Wyoming, hoping to start over—something most women of the time wouldn't have tried. She settling in the railroad town of Rawlins and once again found a job as a cook and a seamstress in a boarding house, one of the few opportunities available to women.

Rawlins was near the railroad and the Oregon Trail.

Ella had her freedom, safety, and self-respect working as a cook, but maybe she dreamed of something more, like a home of her own. In 1885, at age 24, she met James "Jim" Averell. He was a successful businessman homesteading on rangeland along the Sweetwater River between Rawlins and Casper. The old Oregon Trail passed through the area, and though immigrants usually traveled by train in the 1880s, the route was still important for cowboys and other travelers.

"There are opportunities out there," he told Ella.

That caught her interest. "What kind of opportunities?"

"Lots of travelers coming through, looking for a place to stay and a nice meal. I can sell them canned beans, but I bet they'd pay a lot for a meal like you cook."

Jim Averell convinced Ella to come cook for him, but William Pickle had made her cautious, and she wanted to maintain some independence. In 1886, she claimed squatter's rights on the parcel of land next to his, the first step toward filing for a homestead. They had both picked prime pieces of land, near the trails, the railroad, and water, and they prospered for a while.

Jim and Ella's relationship also prospered, and Ella applied for a marriage license in 1886. But one of the first mysteries about Ella comes from this marriage license, because she took out the license, but never returned it with proof of the marriage. Did she get cold feet and decide not to marry Jim? Did she want to wait longer? Or, were they married in secret?

They might have had a reason for a secret marriage: if Ella was a married woman, she would lose her homestead, since married couples could only have one homestead between them. By pretending to be single, Ella could keep her land. She filed for a homestead claim on her 160 acres in 1888, so if she and Jim didn't marry in secret, maybe they were waiting to marry until she owned the land outright in five years. Either way, Ella continued to cook for Jim's ranch, but she also went to work setting up fences for her own cattle operations.

A view of the rangeland along the Sweetwater River in Wyoming. Photo courtesy of the US Department of the Interior.

Ella and Jim may or may not have been skirting the homesteading rules with a secret marriage, but their claims on two prime pieces of land didn't go unnoticed.

Ella started getting visits from Albert "A.J." Bothwell, one of the most powerful ranchers in Wyoming. He was a prominent member of a group of wealthy cattle barons in Wyoming who worked together to keep smaller ranchers out, called the Wyoming Stock Growers Association or WSGA. They didn't own the public range land, but they acted like they did. Bothwell was always trying to put up fences illegally on Ella's land, and when she tore them down, he started applying more pressure on her.

"Why don't you sell your land to me?" Bothwell asked Ella.

"This is my homestead."

"My cattle need the water on this land. I was using it before you got here."

"Then you should have settled it." She thought it over. "But until I get my own cattle, you can pay to use my water."

This made Bothwell furious. "Fine, but you will regret this."

It didn't take long before Ella saw Bothwell put his promise into action. She needed to buy cattle—just a few to start her herd. None of the members of the WSGA would sell to her. She thought she might claim some of the stray calves called mavericks that often wandered the range in the spring. But the WSGA had a law passed that to buy unclaimed cattle, you had to have a registered brand to mark your cattle and tell them apart from other people's cattle. The fees to register a brand were high, but Ella had saved money working at the boarding house and then with Jim, so she applied for a brand. The WSGA made sure they had a say in whose brand was approved, and Ella's was quickly rejected. She tried five different brands in 1888, and each time, her brand application was denied.

Cattle brands like these from Texas helped tell ranchers'
animals apart. Photo courtesy of Billy Hathorn, CC 3.0.

Ella was frustrated, and she complained to a neighbor, John Crowder, a small rancher who had lost his wife and was struggling to keep his ranch and his family together.

"I'm stuck until I can get a brand, and they're not going to let me have one."

John Crowder thought it over. "My ranch isn't doing too good. I'll sell you my brand."

Ella agreed. Because Crowder's L-U brand was already registered, Ella didn't have to get approval from the WSGA to use it. She also took in John's eleven-year-old son Gene. Maybe that was part of the deal: she got the brand if she took in the boy whose father couldn't care for him. Or maybe she felt bad for John and Gene and was trying to help them both. She had a reputation for kindness to her neighbors, and they said no one went hungry when Ella was around to feed them.

With her L-U brand, Ella could now buy cattle, but the WSGA still wasn't going to sell her any. Ella found another way to get the cows she needed. Travelers on the Oregon and Mormon Trails sometimes brought cattle with them, and if the cattle weren't doing well on the trip, or if the immigrants were running low on money, they might sell the animals on the way. Ella was able to buy 28 sickly cows from immigrants to start her ranch in late 1888.

By the spring of 1889, Ella's herd had grown to 41 cattle. It's possible that some of the cows she bought in 1888 had produced calves, but she also might have found a way to gather maverick calves off the range out from under the WSGA's noses.

Ella might have broken the law by taking the mavericks, but if she did, she likely felt justified because it was an unfair law set up by an unjust system. She wouldn't have been the only female rancher to defy big cattle corporations. Shortly after the time of Ella's murder, the Bassett Sisters, Ann and Josie, ran a cattle ranch on the border of Colorado and Utah in defiance of the big cattle companies. They survived the pressure of the big ranchers in part because they were friends with Butch Cassidy's outlaw gang, the Wild Bunch, who protected them from the big companies' agents. The Bassett Sisters also were rumored to rustle cattle from the big ranchers at times, though they were never convicted.

We don't know if Ella rustled the cattle or not. But unlike the Bassett sisters—and despite what A.J. Bothwell and the WSGA would later claim—she wasn't friends with any outlaws. In fact, her ranch became a haven for people in trouble. She was popular with her neighbors and known as a kind-hearted woman who tried to take care of others.

Mingled with her kind-heartedness, though, was toughness. She didn't let people bully her around, especially not Bothwell and the WSGA. And neither did Jim. Bothwell and other members of the WSGA tried to sell plots of land in a Wyoming town that didn't exist, to trick money out of new settlers. They also set up homesteads under fake names to grab up more land. Jim was angry that they were trying to trick people. Or, maybe he was tired of the WSGA running the show. He and Ella may or may not have bent the rules themselves, but he was the postmaster and a justice of the peace, so people would listen to him. He wrote letters to the papers exposing the WSGA's fraud.

Jim Averell, as postmaster, spoke out against the WSGA.
Photo courtesy of Wikimedia.

Bothwell started sending some of his men to watch Jim and Ella. They usually didn't do anything, just stood around watching with their guns in their holsters, making it clear that Bothwell had his eye on the couple.

Ella came home one day to find a skull and crossbones painted on her door. She washed it off, figuring that, especially because she was a woman, Bothwell wouldn't dare actually hurt her. She didn't understand how much Bothwell wanted to destroy her.

In July of 1889, a detective hired by Bothwell snuck over to Ella's ranch and claimed to see Ella branding stolen calves. We don't know if the calves were really stolen, but the accusation was all Bothwell needed to finally rid himself of two thorns in his side: Ella and Jim. He gathered a gang from the WSGA, and they set out to capture the couple.

They caught Ella at her house. The men surrounded the cabin with guns pointed at the windows and they pounded the door.

"What do you want?" Ella called.

"We're taking you into town to be tried as a cattle thief."

"I haven't done anything wrong."

"We have a warrant, so you'd better come along quietly."

Ella opened the door. Gene Crowder tried to run for help.

"Not so fast there!" One of the men held him back, and he had to watch as the men forced Ella onto a wagon. Soon after, another group of WSGA men brought Jim along. They'd pulled him off his wagon on his way to town.

What the men didn't know was that one of Ella's neighbors, Frank Buchanan, had seen the men surround Ella's house. He followed at a distance to see what they were going to do.

The wagon soon turned away from the road to town and out to a gully near Independence Rock and the Sweetwater River. The WSGA gang pulled out their ropes.

Realizing that the men were planning a lynching, Buchanan fired at them. He hit at least one of the men and fired until he ran out of bullets, but he was out manned and out gunned, so he ran to go get help.

He would be too late.

"Don't do this!" Ella said. "If you have mothers or daughters, imagine how you would want them to be treated."

But the men didn't listen. They tied the ropes around Ella and Jim's necks as the two fought to escape. The WSGA didn't plan a real hanging, where the person falls and the jolt usually breaks the person's neck and kills them quickly. They tied the ropes to the branch of a tree and drove the wagon away, leaving Ella and Jim hanging. The two flailed and fought the ropes, trying to get free, until they strangled to death.

Frank Buchanan, Gene Crowder, and other witnesses who worked on or near Ella's ranch went to the sheriff, and Bothwell and his men were arrested and brought under investigation. But the newspapers, backed by the WSGA, were quick to put out false stories about Jim and Ella. No longer did Wyoming newspapers laugh at the "fiction" of the Cattle Kate stories. They swapped Ella's life with that of Cattle Kate, saying she was a cussing, sharp-shooting leader of a band of thieves. And where newspapers didn't claim that Ella was a notorious desperado, they said instead that she was a filthy, cowardly woman who couldn't even ride a horse, a dupe of Jim Averell.

Jim, a former solider, had once shot a man in self-defense, so the newspapers made him out to be a cowardly murderer. The stories couldn't agree on the details of the hanging, and made up most of the story, right down to the type of tree the pair were hung from. The only thing the stories agreed on was that the killing was justified and would discourage future cattle thieves.

Given the influence the WSGA and Bothwell had over the papers, it would be interesting to know if they had anything to do with the earlier Cattle Kate stories. Bothwell may have

MYSTERIES OF THE OLD WEST

wanted to make Wyoming sound exciting to the people he was trying to trick into moving into his made-up town. Or, maybe he was already planning to kill Ella in early 1889 and wanted to use the story as a cover. Unless the author of the Cattle Kate stories is ever discovered, we'll never know if there was a connection.

Meanwhile, rumors circulated among Jim and Ella's neighbors that anyone who testified against Bothwell would meet the same fate. Bothwell was even said to point out good hanging trees to anyone who opposed him.

Eleven-year-old Gene Crowder vanished. Some believed that his father sent him away for his protection, but to this day, no one knows what became of him.

The neighbor Frank Buchanan went missing as well, apparently on the run and in hiding from Bothwell. Some years later, human bones were found with some possessions that might have been Buchanan's. If they were Buchanan's remains, we may never know if Buchanan met with an accident while in hiding, or if Bothwell and the WSGA caught up with him.

Despite all the threats and disappearances, Jim's 20-year-old nephew Ralph Cole was willing to testify against Bothwell. He had worked for Jim and Ella. Maybe he had heard the WSGA men lie about having a warrant or knew about the skull and crossbones threat painted on the door. He might have had evidence that the calves Ella was branding weren't stolen. Either way, he represented a threat to Bothwell and his WSGA cronies.

On the day of the trial, Ralph began to feel ill. Before the trial started, he was dead. His body was hurriedly buried.

When the county coroner, a man named Bennett, heard about the sudden death and burial, he ordered the body exhumed.

After examining the body, he said, "I believe there has been foul play. The boy may have been poisoned."

Despite the coroner's findings, Ralph's death was never investigated.

With all the witnesses conveniently dead or missing, the trial against Bothwell was thrown out, and Bothwell was eventually able to crossbones claim Kate and Jim's homesteads. Bothwell's actions led to what has been called the Range Wars of the 1890s, where a group of small ranchers banded together to fight against the WSGA. Some of Bothwell's gang were killed by other members of the WSGA, perhaps to keep them silent about their actions regarding Jim and Ella. Other members were killed by the small ranchers in their fight over the rangeland.

A few of the killers, including Bothwell, retired as wealthy men, though Bothwell is later said to have lost his mind, perhaps a fitting end for someone who certainly must have had blood on his hands. Even if Ella and Jim had committed crimes, they deserved a fair trial and not a lynching, and the questions remain about what happened to Frank Buchanan, Ralph Cole, Gene Crowder, and other witnesses to the lynching.

The details about what happened have been lost, especially because of the false stories spread by the newspapers paid off by the WSGA. In fact, for many years the newspapers' stories of Cattle Kate were accepted as fact except by family members and friends of the couple, who passed down what they remembered of the real events. Only recently have historians digging into the story discovered the lies and started to unwrap them, bringing a measure of justice to Ella Watson and James Averell, but leaving us with many questions about their deaths and the deaths of their friends.

11

THE FINAL RESTING PLACE OF BUTCH CASSIDY AND THE SUNDANCE KID

In the 1960s, the days of the Wild West seemed long ago, but at least one person kept their memories alive: Josie Bassett, almost 90 years old, had once been known as an outlaw queen along with her sister Ann. Josie and Ann had run a cattle ranch on the borders of Utah, Colorado, and Wyoming, and had likely engaged in some cattle rustling themselves. Josie had been a bootlegger making alcohol when it was banned in the US during Prohibition in the 1920s, and some people said she had poisoned her fifth husband when she got tired of him. Still, during the Great Depression she had helped her neighbors by poaching meat to feed hungry families, and in her later years, she liked to tell them stories about the wild days of the Old West.

She had plenty of stories about the outlaw Butch Cassidy and his gang, the Wild Bunch. She would know, since she dated several of the men in her younger days. In addition to stealing horses and robbing stagecoaches, they also had a reputation for being sort of "Robin Hoods" of the Old West, showing up at local dances with their best manners and helping out poor neighbors. That was until Butch Cassidy and the Sundance Kid had been killed in a shootout in Bolivia while hiding from American law officers. But the elderly Josie had a claim wilder than any of her other stories: Butch hadn't died in the shootout. Instead, he had stuck back into the US and lived out his days in peaceful retirement. Was Josie just spinning yarns to entertain her neighbors? Or had one of America's most famous outlaws faked his own death?

Butch Cassidy had been born in Utah as Robert LeRoy "Roy" Parker. His parents were Latter-day Saint immigrants from England, and they worked a ranch in central Utah. When Roy was thirteen, he went off on his own to work at a ranch. He befriended a local cattle rustler named Mike Cassidy, who taught him how to shoot a gun and handle horses. Roy would later take his hero's last name as his own, while the nickname "Butch" came from working at a butcher's shop in Wyoming.

One story says that Cassidy's first encounter with the law came when he was still a teen. He needed a new pair of overalls, but the store was closed, so he broke in, took the overalls and a pie, and left a note promising to pay for them later. The shop owner wasn't impressed and had him arrested. Maybe that was when Cassidy first decided it wasn't worth being honest.

Either way, Cassidy started getting involved in cattle rustling. He also took honest jobs from time to time, moving to Colorado, Wyoming, and Montana. In 1889, he robbed a bank in Telluride, Colorado—his first known move to bank robbery.

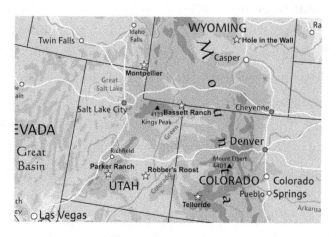

Butch Cassidy's activities ranged all throughout the Intermountain West.

Cassidy bought a ranch in Wyoming, and also found a perfect hideout elsewhere in the state called Hole in the Rock. His ranch wasn't very successful, though, and his outlaw business ran into trouble when he was arrested for stealing cattle in 1894. He spent a year and a half in jail and was released for good behavior in 1896.

His good behavior didn't last long. That same year, Cassidy and his best friend Elzy Lay started their outlaw gang, first called the Hole in the Rock Gang and then the Wild Bunch. Cassidy bragged that they were going to be less violent outlaws and that he had never killed a man or woman, though other members of his gang did. They recruited other outlaws with names like The Tall Texan and Kid Curry, and even a woman, Laura Bullion, whose father had been an outlaw and who had been dating The Tall

Texan. They also invited Harry Alonzo Longabaugh, who was better known as the Sundance Kid for stealing horses in Sundance, Wyoming.

The Wild Bunch. Butch Cassidy is on the far right. Photo courtesy of Wikimedia.

The gang's first job was a robbery in Montpelier, Idaho, near the borders of Utah and Wyoming. Soon, they began their spree of bank and train robberies, becoming the most notorious—and most successful—train robbers in the American West. The only job they ever did in Cassidy's native Utah was the robbery of a mining company's payroll. Their biggest job was a $70,000 robbery of a Rio Grande train in New Mexico.

Cassidy had a reputation for helping smaller ranchers, such as the Bassett sisters, especially against the big ranching corporations. Perhaps because his father had lost part of his ranch in a land dispute. His gang also showed up at community dances and other social events, with their best manners ready to dance with the local girls. They were celebrities.

But their fame also brought a massive hunt to capture

the outlaws. The Pinkerton Detectives, famous bounty hunters, had wanted posters and information on all of the Wild Bunch. The Wild Bunch was good at scattering after a job, and then they would meet up at Hole in the Rock in Wyoming or Robber's Roost in central Utah. In 1899, some of the gang members robbed a train in New Mexico without Cassidy. One of the men, Ketchum, was killed, and Cassidy's best friend, Elzy Lay, was wounded and sent to prison.

Maybe that was a turning point for Cassidy. In 1900, Cassidy tried to convince the governor of Utah to grant the gang amnesty—a pardon for their crimes—if they went straight. A few months later, apparently having given up that idea, they were reported in Nevada robbing a bank. Then, the Sundance Kid fled to New York and married his mysterious sweetheart, who went by the name Ethel or Etta Place.

Wedding photo of the Sundance Kid and Etta Place. Etta's real name and origin are a mystery. She bears a strong resemblance to "Outlaw Queen" Ann Bassett, leading some to wonder if they are the same person, though it would have meant she was somehow running ranches in Utah and Argentina at the same time. Photo courtesy of Wikimedia.

Early in 1901, Butch Cassidy, the Sundance Kid, and Etta Place, escaped to South America and took up ranching in Argentina. In fact, thanks to a change in land laws in the country, Etta was the first woman to own land in Argentina.

Ranching seemed to go well for a while, but the Pinkerton Detectives didn't let distance stop them. In 1905, the group sold their ranch and fled before the detectives reached them. Etta sailed back to San Francisco, and Cassidy and Sundance laid low in Chile and Bolivia.

Without ranching to support themselves, they fell back on their old profession. There were a number of American outlaws hiding out in South America, and it's hard to say which robberies were done by Cassidy and Sundance, but they certainly robbed a few banks.

In 1908, A pair of American men robbed the payroll of a silver mine. They then went to lay low in San Vicente, Bolivia. But the residents were suspicious and notified the authorities, who engaged in a gun fight with the two men. One of the outlaws was mortally injured, and it seemed that his companion shot him to end his suffering and then shot himself instead of being captured. The authorities compared the bodies to the wanted posters and descriptions circulated by the Pinkerton Detective Agency and declared that the two outlaws were Butch Cassidy and the Sundance Kid.

Cassidy and Sundance had robbed payrolls before, but they weren't the only ones. The two outlaws matched their descriptions. And a woman matching the description of Etta Place showed up in Bolivia and asked for Sundance's death certificate.

But there were rumors. Josie Bassett wasn't the only one

who claimed to see Butch Cassidy in the US after his death. His sister later claimed that she had seen him as well, and that he moved to Washington and died there in 1937.

A man named William Henry Long moved to Duchesne, Utah—near the Wild Bunch's old hangout—after Longabaugh's supposed death in Bolivia. He was secretive about his past, and most of the local residents were convinced he was an outlaw hiding from the law. He died of a gunshot wound in 1936. Was Long the same man as Longabaugh?

Etta Place also disappeared from history after 1909, just as mysteriously as she had appeared.

It would not be unheard of for former outlaws to create a new identity and a new life after their bank robbing days were over. Laura Bullion was arrested for train robbery and spent almost four years in prison before getting her second chance.

Mug shot of Laura Bullion after her capture by the Pinkerton Detectives. Photo courtesy of Wikimedia.

When Bullion was released, she moved to Tennessee, changed her name to Freda Bullion Lincoln, claimed she was a widow, and worked as a seamstress. She died in 1961—the last member of the Wild Bunch to pass away. Josie Bassett outlived her by only two years.

Elzy Lay didn't change his name, but he was released from prison for helping to save the warden's wife and daughter when they were taken hostage during a prison riot. He visited the Bassett sisters in Utah but settled in California where he married, ran a business, and raised two children.

And rumors had swirled that outlaw Billy the Kid, shot in New Mexico in 1881, had somehow survived, despite the fact that a jury of men had witnessed his body.

Some people believe that outlaw Billy the Kid faked his death. Image courtesy of Wikimedia.

But did Cassidy and Longabaugh do the same? In an attempt to end the debate, researchers collected DNA from their living relatives. They returned to the cemetery in San Vicente and exhumed the bodies suspected to be the two outlaws. The DNA did not match. Uncertain about the exact resting places of the outlaws, they tested several other bodies, and none of them matched.

Researchers also exhumed the body of William Henry Long in Duchesne, Utah. But that body did not match the DNA of the Sundance Kid's relative either. If Longabaugh survived Bolivia and returned to the US, he hid his tracks well. Perhaps along with Etta Place?

If Butch Cassidy returned to the US, no one agrees on where he lived and died. His sister claimed he died in Washington. Many people in southern Nevada said he turned to mining—sometimes with his old friend Elzy Lay—and died there. Others in central Utah claim he returned to the old family homestead in his final days.

Josie Bassett might have known the truth. After Laura Bullion died in 1961, Josie was the last living connection to the Wild Bunch. She insisted that she'd seen Butch Cassidy after his death. Maybe she was just spinning yarns, but maybe she was telling the truth and knew where her old flame had settled down in his honest years. She was kicked by a horse in 1963 and, at the age of 90, died of her injuries, taking the last of the Wild Bunch's secrets with her.

12

ALASKA'S CAVE OF SECRETS

In 1899, the Alaskan Gold Rush was on, and all the news out of Yukon, Canada and Alaska was gold, gold, gold. But a steamboat captain named D.C. Bayse wrote to the papers about another treasure he and his shipmates discovered in Alaska: a forgotten civilization. No one at the time was interested in history when they thought of the fortunes waiting to be made in the goldfield, so Bayse's claims got little attention, and the mystery his crew uncovered has been lost to us once again.

Early European explorers and fur trappers in Alaska and the Yukon had heard rumors of gold in the area, but the furs were more profitable and less work than panning for gold in the frigid Yukon waters. In the 1880s, a series of gold discoveries brought some miners to Alaska. And in 1896, Native Tagish siblings "Skookum" Jim Mason and Kate Carmack, along with Kate's Anglo-American husband George Carmack and Jim and Kate's nephew Dawson Charlie found gold in Rabbit Creek off the Klondike River—so much gold layered between rocks that it looked like cheese sandwiches. When the news reached the rest of the United States in 1897, it triggered a huge gold rush.

Hopeful miners climbing Chilkoot Pass. The steps carved into the snow and ice were sometimes called the Golden Staircase. Photo courtesy of the Library of Congress.

Over 100,000 people attempted to reach the Klondike that summer. The Canadian government required them to bring enough food for one year so they wouldn't starve to death in the frigid, snowy environment, which meant that each person was bringing almost a ton—2,000 pounds—of food and mining supplies.

Most miners opted to make the massive climb over Chilkoot or White Pass, which required multiple trips to bring their supplies over the pass. But those who had a little money to spend could take the longer but faster and easier way of going up the Yukon River by boat all the way across Alaska and up to Dawson City. D.C. Bayse was the captain of the steamboat *Oil City*, one of the boats that made the long, dangerous journey up the Yukon.

*The two main routes to the Klondike gold fields were to go
through southern Alaska and over the steep passes, or to
take a boat farther north and follow the Yukon River across
Alaska and into Canada. Image courtesy of Wikimedia.*

In October of 1898, when the *Oil City* was on the Yukon near the Alaskan town of Russian Mission, Bayse saw signs of ice in the river. It was early for the river to freeze over, but Bayse was worried. Once the river froze for the winter, it would be too icy to travel for six months. He found a side stream near Russian Mission, and the men on the boat prepared for a long, cold winter near the Arctic Circle where the sun barely rose above the horizon for months at a time.

They had some provisions on board their steamship, but with little to do and little to eat, the men sometimes went out hunting when the weather was clear. There wasn't much to catch, but they sometimes found grouse or rabbits.

On one of these hunting trips, Captain Bayse went out with the ship's steward, a Chinese immigrant named Lin Que. As the steward, Lin was in charge of food and supplies. They decided to venture farther into the icy wilderness than usual, hoping to find meat to bring back to the ship. They climbed a high ridge and found a sort of valley among the rocks. Captain Bayse sat down to rest after the difficult hike, but Lin explored a little further.

Lin spotted what looked like a large animal den in the

rocks. He had to duck to fit through the narrow entrance, but he sneaked inside, his ears alert for any sounds of wild animals, but it was so dark past the entrance that he couldn't tell how far the cave went or what was inside it. He hurried back out.

"Captain!" he called. "Come along quick! There's a huge hole in these rocks."

Captain Bayse scrambled up after Lin, and he peered inside as well.

"We haven't seen any bears," the captain said, "and I don't care to look for any in so dangerous a place."

He thought for a minute, maybe considering the ship's lack of meat, then handed Lin his revolver. "Back me up."

Bayse raised his Winchester rifle and fired several times into the caves. The echoes bounced back to them, stinging their ears, as loud as cannon shot. Both men raised their guns and waited for some angry animal to charge out at them.

Nothing stirred in the cave.

"Should we go in?" Lin asked.

Bayse grunted his agreement, and they cleared away the debris from an old rock slide to widen the entrance. They used a stick and some cloth to make a sort of torch and then ducked through the opening of the cave.

"You go first," Bayse ordered Lin.

The steward wasn't happy, but he took the torch and the revolver and wiggled his way through the narrow opening until it widened into a room about twenty feet wide. In the center was a stone that was set up like a table. The ash from an old fire in one corner showed that they weren't the first humans to view this room.

The room opened into another that looked even bigger. The torch reflected off something in the bigger room: six glittered points. Lin swung the torch around to reveal three bears watching the men.

The first bear charged for Captain Bayse. He raised his rifle and fired, killing the bear with one lucky shot.

Lin was less lucky. His revolver wasn't big enough to kill a bear—even a young one—and after one shot, he tossed the revolver and torch aside and drew the knife he carried. The bear leaped on him, biting his arm as he stabbed it. Bayse tried to find a good shot, but he couldn't shoot the bear without the risk of hitting Lin as well. Bayse shot the third bear instead, and Lin managed to kill the bear he was wrestling with, though his arms were badly bitten.

The torch was almost out now. Bayse wiped his forehead. "We'd better go back. Send some men with a dog sled to bring the meat back."

Now that the animals were dead, they weren't going to waste the meat. It would feed them for quite a while.

They made their way back to the ship, and Lin got his arms cleaned and bandaged. Both men were still curious about the cave they had discovered. Who had lived there in the past? When another stretch of good weather presented itself, they decided to go back. They stuffed their thick socks and shoes with straw for extra warmth, and they loaded a sled with an oil stove, enough food for several days, and warm wool blankets.

It took them five hours to haul their sled back to the cave

in the bitter cold, and they were exhausted by the time they got there. Lin set up the oil stove and cooked something to warm them up, which they ate at the ancient stone table.

By the extra light of their oil lamps, they began to notice more about the cave. Bayse thought he spotted cave paintings on the walls under the layers of dirt and ancient soot. They used the straw from their boots to carefully clean the walls, and they uncovered an astonishing set of drawings painted in red on the light-colored walls.

The drawings seemed to tell the story of three boats or canoes of people leaving from their home and crossing a sea filled with whales, seals, and walruses and sailed up a river. Perhaps the Yukon? The people from the paintings had dogs and hunted deer, moose, buffalo, and bears. Bayse found it strange that there were no sleds or other indications of snow in the paintings. If, as seemed likely, these paintings told the story of people who had come from somewhere in Asia to Alaska to settle or hunt, why did they not have any drawings of the snow? Was Alaska warmer in the past? Or, had they been somewhere father south and somehow become stranded in Alaska, and used the painting to record their previous lives? They clearly wanted to leave a record of their adventures, but it was hard to know what story they were telling.

In the larger room in the back, Bayse and Lin discovered that the walls had been carved with sea monsters and other strange animals, as well as stars—perhaps an ancient map of the skies. A set of what looked like bunkbeds had also been carved into the wall. They found a few other remnants in the room. One was a coin that looked Chinese, with a square hole in the center, but Lin didn't recognize it and guessed it must be very old. They also found bones that looked human.

It had already grown dark outside, so Bayse and Lin had to spend the night in the cave. Both had an uneasy sleep. Lin dreamed that he was being chased by ancient Chinese men, and Bayse felt like someone was smothering him in his sleep. It was as if they had disturbed the spirits of the men who had lived in that cave long ago.

When they awoke, they discovered that snow had slid down to cover the entrance to the cave. They were trapped. With limited air and supplies available in the cave, they worked to cut away the ice and snow that blocked their path to freedom. They finally escaped, and they never went back to the cave.

It seems that no one else has ever returned to study the cave and what it means. Other cave paintings done in red ochre have been found in Alaska, but none that match Bayse's description. Does it depict the ancient ancestors of the Native Alaskans making their journey to their new homeland? Or Asian explorers who reached the Americas, perhaps long before Columbus? Did the men—and possibly women—who lived in the cave settle in Alaska and start a new nation there? Did they ever return to the place they had left? Or, did they live out their final days in that cave, lost and far from home? Unless someone discovers its location again, we may never know, and after Bayse and Lin's experience, perhaps the wilderness swallowed the cave under rock and snow slides, keeping its secrets hidden.

13

THE STRANGE MURDER OF FRANK LITTLE

By the early 1900s, the age of the Old West was coming to an end. The bandits had been killed or settled down to honest work, fewer cowboys rode the range, and miners now worked for big companies rather than prospecting on their own. The affordable Model T Ford allowed hordes of Americans to tour long-unmapped parts of the West that once required a treacherous wagon journey.

But an undercurrent of "wild" still lived in the West. It took independent-minded men and women to wrestle resources like coal and timber from hostile deserts and mountains. It also took organization, and, like during the Range Wars, big corporations rose to take control of the men and the money of the West. But the men didn't passively accept the control, and violence was inevitable, as Frank Little would learn.

Little was born in Oklahoma. His mother was part

Cherokee and his father was a Quaker, a member of a Christian religious group that opposed slavery and war. The Littles had settled a homestead in Oklahoma, but the family struggled to grow enough to survive, especially when drought hit. Little's father died in 1899, when Little was twenty, and he decided to move to California with his brother to try his hand at mining. He joined the mining scene just as big changes were on the horizon.

Scofield, Utah was one of the turning points, though Little wasn't there and wouldn't realize it at the time.

On May 1, 1900, John Wilson showed up to work outside the Number 4 shaft of the Winter Quarters Mine in Scofield. He drove a coal cart pulled by a horse, moving the mined coal out of the narrow canyon and down to where trains hauled it to cities for fuel. Driving the cart was not as messy as working in the mines, where the coal dust and grease became so embedded in your hair and skin that you couldn't scrub it all out, and the creases of your fingerprints and palms were always highlighted in black.

At the moment, 300 men and boys were working down in the darkness, blasting more of the mountain away. Some were natives of Utah, but many came from Finland, Wales, and other countries to work for the Pleasant Valley Mine Company. Most had come with their families to Scofield, fathers and sons working together in the mines, with their wives, mothers, and sisters. The mining company owned the wooden shacks where they lived, and the families always owed money to the company stores, which let them buy on credit and then took the money from the men's paychecks.

Children in a Utah coal mining town. Nearly everything in the town would be owned by the mine companies, including the stores and houses. Photo courtesy of the Library of Congress.

Wilson was only twenty, but he was older than a lot of the teenage boys who worked down in the mine shafts, deep under the mountain where it was so dark you could feel the weight of the blackness pressing on you, suffocating you.

A deep rumble groaned far down the throat of the mine. Something hit Wilson—a blast of sound that split his eardrums, and a wall of hot air that upended the cart, killed the horse, and sent Wilson flying 820 feet across the canyon —more than two football fields. He slammed into a tree, cracking open the back of his skull.

People came running from the shacks and wooden buildings of the little town to see what had caused the noise. Wilson survived, though he would never be fully well again. The men and boys in the mine were not so lucky. The blast had crumpled the front of the shaft. Rescuers dug until they cleared the entrance, but the first men who ran in collapsed, unable to breath. Afterdamp, a poisonous combination of gases including carbon monoxide, made the air of the mine toxic.

When enough fresh air had made its way into the shaft, the rescuers were finally able to see the damage. The explosion had burned the miners in the Number 4 shaft so badly many were unrecognizable. The afterdamp had spilled through an air tunnel connecting Number Four to Number One, suffocating the men working in the mine. The rescuers found some still holding their tools. Others were huddled together—fathers with sons, brothers with brothers—where they had fallen fighting for their final breaths.

A few miners had been close enough to the Number One entrance to escape, but the Scofield Mine explosion was, at that point, the worst mining disaster in American history. The company claimed two-hundred men died, but the miners tallied the number of dead or missing family and friends at closer to two-hundred-fifty. Colorado had to send coffins; there were not enough in the state of Utah to bury all the dead men and boys.

Many Scofield families lost multiple family members: fathers, sons, and grandsons all died together in the mines. One woman buried seven sons and three grandsons. Some of the survivors were too badly injured to work. Widows and children were suddenly without an income or even a place to live, since the mining companies only let them keep their houses while their husbands and fathers could work in the mines. The widows even had to buy their husbands' coffins and burial clothes from the company store, but there would be no more paychecks for them.

Imagine how you would feel if you were in Scofield. The mining company had sent the men to work in the mines while the shafts were being blasted, which had placed the miners in danger. Further, the miners had been complaining about a buildup of highly flammable coal dust in the mines. Mining companies were supposed to wet the coal dust down so it wouldn't build up and explode, but the Pleasant Valley Coal Company had not. The coal dust had likely started the explosion, which ignited at least a dozen oversized kegs of black powder stored in the mine shaft.

Yet the company refused to take responsibility for the accident. Many people, from miners to Utah politicians, petitioned the government to help the victims' families— this was before there was any kind of Social Security or unemployment benefits—but the US Congress didn't want to get involved. Citizens around Utah and the rest of the country raised money to help the miners' families. They brought enough pressure on the company that it eventually paid for the funeral costs, erased the victims' debts in the company stores, and gave each widow $500 before sending them on their way.

Scofield was quickly eclipsed by accidents claiming even more lives: at least 362 at Monongah, West Virginia in 1907; 259 in Cherry, Illinois in 1909; 263 in Dawson, New Mexico in 1913. The first decade of the 1900s saw over 150 mining disasters kill nearly 4,000 men and boys. Over 3,000 of those deaths occurred in 1907 alone. Like Scofield, the 1907

Monongah disaster—still the worst in US history—was likely caused by the company not wetting down coal dust.

Miners were willing to do dangerous work—many took pride in it—but they didn't want to take unnecessary risks, and they wanted their families to be cared for if something happened to them. But even after Scofield, neither the government nor the companies offered them the safety nets that they demanded.

Many miners wanted to organize into unions, joining their voices to demand more rights and to go on strike— refusing to work—if the working conditions weren't safe. Mining companies didn't want to lose money or the control over their business, so they refused to allow unions and would hire strikebreakers to attack and beat workers who tried to strike for better conditions. Bloody battles between miners and company bosses exploded across the country.

A conflict between police and union members on strike.
Photo courtesy of Wikimedia.

Into this scene stepped Frank Little.

The dangerous conditions he saw in California and then in Arizona mines, and likely his Quaker background, influenced him to get involved in organizing unions, eventually joining the radical Industrial Workers of the

World (IWW or "Wobblies"). He began to travel across the West—Montana, Washington, California, and elsewhere—encouraging miners, lumberjacks, railway workers, and other laborers to organize and demand better working conditions.

Frank Little faced beatings and jail time in his quest for better working conditions for American laborers. Photo courtesy of the Industrial Workers of the World archives.

Though the First Amendment of the US Constitution guarantees Americans the right to freedom of speech, the big companies often had organizers like Frank Little arrested for speaking up against them. The mine bosses made friends with the police and local politicians and sometimes bribed or threatened them to cooperate. Little was often beaten and threatened by strikebreakers and police for attempting to help workers form unions. In Spokane, Washington, he was arrested for reading the Declaration of Independence in public.

Then, in 1917, the US joined World War I, which had been

ravaging Europe since 1914. Germany's increasing hostility toward the neutral United States—including torpedoing US ships and encouraging Mexico to invade the country—finally drew the nation into war. Everyone feared German spies, and the government and newspapers encouraged people to watch their neighbors and report anyone who spoke against the war.

Many union organizers thought it was wisest to support the war, but Frank Little objected to war just as loudly as he objected to abuses of workers. He saw the two issues as part of the same problem: disregard for the lives of the working class. He called World War I a "rich man's war."

Now, Little had even more enemies—those who hated him for his union efforts and those who thought he was unpatriotic.

Then came the Speculator Mine Disaster in Butte, Montana.

Mines in Butte, Montana. Despite efforts to make them safer, there were still serious problems in the mines that would lead to disaster. Photo courtesy of the Library of Congress.

The Speculator Mine was a copper mine that was important in supporting the war effort. Until a few years previously, the miners in Butte had been protected by a union, but the union had fallen apart due to in-fighting, and the Anaconda Copper Company now ran the town.

On June 8, 1917, an electrical cable broke loose and fell into the mine. Two foremen went down into the shaft to inspect the damage. Though basic battery flashlights had been invented by this time, the foremen carried lanterns with open flames. The electrical cable was wrapped in cloth that had become soaked with oil. When one of the foremen raised his lantern to look at the broken cable, the flame of his lantern ignited the oil. They tried to put the blaze out, but timber frames supported the shafts, and those caught fire. The breeze blowing down the shafts from above pushed the flames into adjoining tunnels.

The horrified foremen hurried back up the mine shaft.

One of them shouted, "For God's sake, get the men out. Get them out!"

But for many of the miners, it was too late. Some died in the fire itself, but many others died slowly, over several days, trapped below the earth as rescue workers unsuccessfully fought the flames and the fire stole their oxygen.

Shift boss J.D. Moore had time to write a series of letters to his wife describing his final hours.

Dear Pet,

This may be the last message you will get from me. The gas broke about 11:15 pm. I tried to get all the men out, but the smoke was too strong. I got some of the boys with me in a drift and put up in a bulkhead. If anything happens to me you better sell the house and go to California and live. You will know your Jim died like a man and his last thoughts were for his wife that I love better than anyone on earth. We'll meet again. Tell mother and the boys goodbye.

With love to my wife and may God take care of you.

Your loving Jim

J.D. Moore

Then later:

Dear Pet,

Well we are waiting for the end. I guess it won't be long. We take turns rapping on the pipe so if the rescue crew is around they will hear us. Well my dear wife try not to worry. I know you will but trust in God everything will come out alright. There's a young fellow here, Clarence Marthy, he has a wife and two kiddies. Tell her we done the best we could but the cards were against us.

Goodbye loving wife

Later still:

All alive but air getting bad, one small piece of candle left.

And his final message:

In the dark.

Several men did survive behind the bulkhead Moore put

up, finally rescued over two days after the fire started, but Moore was one of at least 168 men who died in the disaster.

The remaining miners, furious at the unsafe conditions that led to the fire, went on strike. They were soon joined by electricians, blacksmiths, and other tradesmen. The Anaconda Company tried to divide the striking groups so they wouldn't work together, but Frank Little had heard about the disaster, and he arrived in Butte to help the workers stay organized.

Striking during a war is especially dangerous because it's often seen as unpatriotic. This was the case in Butte, where Little spoke openly against the Anaconda Company and the war. The newspapers denounced him, and the Anaconda Company sent a "home guard" or informal militia to attack the striking workers. Some of the other workers, such as the electricians, reached deals with the company and went back to work by the end of July, but the company refused to make the changes the miners wanted, and the miners' strike continued.

This was the situation in Butte on August 1, 1917 when Frank Little was staying at a boarding house in the city. In the middle of the night, a group of masked men broke into his room. They forced his landlady to show them to Little's room and dragged him out of bed in only his long underwear. They tied him behind a car and dragged him through town to a nearby bridge. His attackers lynched him from the bridge and left him to hang. The noose choked him to death. The autopsy found skin under his fingernails and a fracture in the back of the skull where he had been hit by the butt of a gun. Frank Little had gone down fighting.

The masked attackers left the note pinned to the thigh of his long underwear: "Others take notice, first and last warning, 3-7-77."

No one took credit for the lynching. They didn't have to —they had sent their message.

Despite the warnings, the strike continued on for many months more. Yet there were no other lynchings. It seemed like a personal attack against Little. Perhaps the Anaconda Company saw him as the head of the resistance and thought that removing him would kill the strike. Maybe it wasn't the strike that upset people as much as Little's objections to the war.

Locals had plenty of suspicions and gossip about who had been involved. Dashiell Hammett, who later created the fictional detective Sam Spade, was working for the Pinkerton Detective Agency at the time. He had been sent to Butte to help end the strike, and he later claimed that someone offered him $5,000 to assassinate Little—a huge amount of money. Hammett already disliked strikebreaking, and the incident shook him, causing him to leave his work for Pinkerton, where it seemed people thought he would work as an assassin for hire. Still, some have wondered if he knew more about the lynching than he let on.

One of favorite suspects for the murder was one of the Anaconda Company's strikebreakers named Billy Oates. He already had a reputation for violence. Billy had a hook for a hand, and many thought that some of Little's injuries might have been inflicted by Oates' hook.

Ed Morrissey, Butte's chief detective, was reported to

have scratches on his face after the night of the hanging, and he disappeared from town for a while after Little's death.

Another local story claimed that an unnamed group of men who were suspected of being involved in the lynching all died together in a suspicious car accident, maybe to cover up what they knew about the murder.

But no one was ever charged with the lynching of Frank Little.

The 3-7-77 remains mysterious as well. It is a number that was used by a group of Montana vigilantes in the 1800s. These vigilantes formed posses in the absence of organized police to chase down outlaws. Some people think the numbers are the dimensions of a grave: 3 feet by 7 feet by 77 inches. It could represent the amount of time a person had to get out of town. Others think it's associated with a Masonic temple in Bannack, Montana that was founded March 7, 1877, and which a number of important citizens and probably some of the vigilantes belonged to. The exact meaning of the number is lost (or still a secret), though it appears on Montana police badges today.

Whatever the meaning of 3-7-77, the original Montana vigilantes were gone by the time of Little's murder; their heyday was between the 1860s and 1880s. It's not clear if Little's murderers were associated with another formal vigilante group or the police, or if they saw themselves as carrying on the vigilantes' role of enforcing their idea of order. Unless someone discovers who the murderers were, we may never know the significance of the message.

Frank Little's funeral drew thousands of people—the largest funeral ever held in Butte. But after that, the federal government cracked down on protesters throughout the West, slowing the efforts of many laborers to form unions or get safer working conditions. Frank Little was largely forgotten as the sun set on the Old West, and the secrets of his murder are now lost to time.

SELECTED SOURCES AND
FURTHER READINGS

EMPTY VILLAGES IN THE CLIFFS

Gustaf Nordenskiold, *The Cliff Dwellers of the Mesa Verde*, Mesa Verde Museum Association, reprint of 1893 edition.

David Roberts, *In Search of the Old Ones*, Simon Schuster, 1997.

ESTEBAN THE MOOR AND THE SEVEN CITIES OF GOLD

Álvar Núñez Cabeza de Vaca, translated by Cyclone Covey, *Cabeza de Vaca's Adventures in the Unknown Interior of America*, Hispaniola Books, 2016, translated from 1542 edition.

Dedra McDonald Birzer, "Esteban," BlackPast.org

National Park Service, "Esteban de Dorantes,"

https://www.nps.gov/coro/learn/historyculture/esteban-de-
dorantes.htm

THE LOST HAWAIIAN TRAPPERS

Jean Barman, *Leaving Paradise: Indigenous Hawaiians in the
Pacific Northwest, 1787-1898*, University of Hawaii Press, 2006.
    George I. Quimby, "Hawaiians in the Fur Trade of North-
West America, 1785-1829," *The Journal of Pacific History*
(Volume 7, 1972).
    Alexander Ross, *The Fur Hunters of the Far West, Volume
One* (London: Smith, Elder and Co, 1855).

THE MYSTERIOUS WEALTH OF THOMAS RHOADES

Lee Davidson, "Legends of Utah Gold," *Deseret News*,
November 26, 1989.
    J. Kenneth Davies, "Mormons and California Gold,"
Journal of Mormon History, Volume 7 (1980): 83-99.
    J. Kenneth Davies, "Thomas Rhoads, Forgotten Mormon
Pioneer of 1846," *Nebraska History* 64 (1983): 81-95
    Richard Markosian, "Lost Rhoades Mine How to Find It,"
Utah Stories, August 2013.
    Michael Riley, "Glittering bits of legend draw dreamers
to Utah," *The Denver Post*, July 30, 2016.
    Stephen B. Shaffer, *Out of the Dust: Utah's Lost Mines and
Treasures*, Cedar Fort: 2006.
    Twila Van Leer, "Rhoads, Gold Seemed to go Hand in
Hand," *Deseret News*, July 2, 1996.

THE TATTOOED GIRL

Margot Mifflin, *The Blue Tattoo*, University of Nebraska Press, 2009.

Cecilia Rasmussen, "Tale of Kindness Didn't Fit Notion of Savage Indian," *Los Angeles Times*, July 16, 2000.

Royal Stratton and Charles Rivers Editors, *The Captivity of the Oatman Girls*, Charles River Editors edition, 2017.

THE OUTLAWS' HIDDEN LOOT

Denver Library Blog, "The Reynolds Gang: Colorado Confederates and Their Buried Treasure."

D.J. Cook, *Hands Up or Thirty-five Years of Detective Life in the Mountains and on the Plains*, Project Gutenberg Edition, 2013.

Jeff Eberle, "The Reynolds Gang," *Colorado Encyclopedia*, https://coloradoencyclopedia.org/article/reynolds-gang

THE LOST COMPANY OF THE LITTLE BIGHORN

Thom Hatch, "George Armstrong Custer," *Essential Civil War Curriculum*, https://www.essentialcivilwarcurriculum.com/george-armstrong-custer.html

Thomas Powers, "How the Battle of Little Bighorn was Won," *Smithsonian Magazine*, November 2010.

John V. Quarstein, "Up, Up and Away: Civil War Ballooning in Hampton Roads," *Mariners' Blog*, The Mariners' Museum and Park, November 12, 2020.

Jim Robbins, "A Fresh Look at the Last Stand," *Chicago Tribune,* January 18, 1986.

Robert M. Utley, *Little Bighorn Battlefield: A History and Guide to the Battle of Little Bighorn,* National Park Service, 1988.

THE MURDER OF DI LEE

Grant K. Anderson, "Deadwood's Chinatown," *South Dakota State Historical Society,* 1975.

Jerry Bryant and Bill Markley, "Death of Deadwood's China Doll," *Historynet,* June 20, 2017.

Bill Markley, "Deadwood's Lost Chinatown," *True West,* June 1, 2006.

THE CURSED TREASURE OF THE SUPERSTITION MOUNTAINS

Bob Willis, "Has the Lost Dutchman Mine Been Found?" *True West Magazine,* April 2005.

Kathy Weiser, "The Lost Dutchman Mine, Arizona," *Legends of America,* 2019, https://www.legendsofamerica.com/az-lostdutchman/

Tom Kollenborn, *Tom Kollenborn Chronicles,* http://superstitionmountaintomkollenborn.blogspot.com/

Tom Kollenborn and the Superstition Mountain Historical Society, "Jacob Waltz 'Lost Dutchman' Exhibit," Superstition Mountain Museum, https://superstitionmountainmuseum.org/exhibits/jacob-waltz-lost-dutchman-exhibit/

THE LYNCHING OF CATTLE KATE

Jana Bommersbach, "Dead Wrong about Cattle Kate," *True West Magazine*, November 2014.

Daryl Drew, "The Death of Cattle Kate," *Canadian Cowboy Country Magazine*, April/May 2018.

Eliza McGraw, "The Tragedy of Cattle Kate," *Smithsonian Magazine*, March 12, 2018.

THE FINAL RESTING PLACE OF BUTCH CASSIDY AND THE SUNDANCE KID

Nicolas Brulliard, "Wild West Josie," National Parks Conservation Association, Winter 2017.

Chris Enss, "Queen of the Wild Bunch," *True West Magazine*, August 2019.

John Hollenhorst, "DNA evidence shoots holes in Sundance Kid theory," *KSL*, Sept. 15, 2009.

Steven Law, "Butch Cassidy and the Sundance Kid didn't die in a Bolivian Gunfight," *KSL*, Sept 12, 2011.

Bob Mims, "Did Butch Cassidy and Sundance Kid Die in Bolivia? Yes, but..." *Los Angeles Times,* 1996.

W. Paul Reeve, "Just Who Was the Outlaw Queen Etta Place?" *History Blazer*, May 1995.

ALASKA'S CAVE OF SECRETS

D.C. Bayse, "An Alaska Cave," *The Evening Star*, Washington DC, October 13, 1899, accessed at https://explorenorth.com/library/history/an_alaska_cave-1899.html

National Park Service, "What Was the Klondike Gold Rush?" https://www.nps.gov/klgo/learn/goldrush.htm

THE STRANGE MURDER OF FRANK LITTLE

Rory Carroll, "The mysterious lynching of Frank Little," *The Guardian,* 21 Sep 2016.

Kristen Inbody, "'No greater love:' Heroes emerged in Butte's darkest hours," *Great Falls Tribune*, May 26, 2017.

J.D. Moore, "Letters," The Speculor Miners' last letters, accessed at https://libcom.org/article/speculator-miners-last-letters

Allan Kent Powell, *The Next Time We Strike: Labor in Utah's Coal Fields,* Logan: Utah State University Press, 1985.

ALSO BY E.B. WHEELER

Non-fiction:

Utah Women: Pioneers, Poets & Politicians

Utah Fiction:

The Bone Map (for middle grade readers)

No Peace with the Dawn (with Jeffery Bateman)

Bootleggers and Basil (in *The Pathways to the Heart*)

Letters from the Homefront

Balm of the Heart (in *In the Valley)*

Blood in a Dry Town (Tenny Mateo Mystery)

British Fiction:

The Haunting of Springett Hall

Born to Treason

The Royalist's Daughter

Wishwood (Westwood Gothic)

Moon Hollow (Westwood Gothic)

Young Readers:

Alejandra the Axolotl and the Big Mess

ACKNOWLEDGMENTS

Thank you to my critique groups, The Writers' Cache and UPSSEFW, and to my beta readers, Alex, Claire, Dan, Karen, and Zoey, for their feedback and taking some of the mystery out of writing. Abigail Samoun gave me early feedback that was useful in developing this collection of stories. And as always, I couldn't do this without the understanding, patience, and support of my family.

ABOUT THE AUTHOR

E.B. Wheeler attended BYU, majoring in history with an English minor, and earned graduate degrees in history and landscape architecture from Utah State University. She's the award-winning author of over a dozen books, including *The Bone Map, Utah Women: Pioneers, Poets & Politicians,* and Whitney Award finalists *A Proper Dragon* and *Born to Treason,* as well as several short stories, magazine articles, and scripts for educational software programs for young people. The League of Utah Writers named her the Writer of the Year in 2016. In addition to writing, she consults about historic preservation and teaches history. She's always loved Indian Jones and hopes to someday find a lost treasure.

Find more about her and her books at ebwheeler.com

Printed in the USA
CPSIA information can be obtained
at www.ICGtesting.com
LVHW012352271123
764922LV00005B/358